Must the Chinese Go?

Also from Westphalia Press
westphaliapress.org

Must the Chinese Go?

An Examination of the Chinese Question

by Mrs. S. L. Baldwin

WESTPHALIA PRESS
An imprint of Policy Studies Organization

Must the Chinese Go?: An Examination of the Chinese Question
All Rights Reserved © 2015 by Policy Studies Organization

Westphalia Press
An imprint of Policy Studies Organization
1527 New Hampshire Ave., NW
Washington, D.C. 20036
info@ipsonet.org

ISBN-13: 978-1-63391-225-0
ISBN-10: 1633912256

Cover design by Jeffrey Barnes:
jbarnesdesign.com

Daniel Gutierrez-Sandoval, Executive Director
PSO and Westphalia Press

Updated material and comments on this edition
can be found at the Westphalia Press website:
www.westphaliapress.org

MUST THE CHINESE GO?

AN

EXAMINATION OF THE CHINESE QUESTION.

BY

MRS. S. L. BALDWIN.

EIGHTEEN YEARS A MISSIONARY IN CHINA.

THIRD EDITION.

PREFACE TO THE SECOND EDITION

A PORTION of this pamphlet was published, and quite widely circulated, at the time when the first anti-Chinese law was pending in Congress. Although a Republican Congress, Republicans and Democrats, with a few noble exceptions, united in the insult to a friendly but weaker nation, and, in defiance of the whole spirit of our Constitution and loyalty to God, passed the iniquitous law.

In view of the late terrible massacre of Chinese in the West, and the repeated requests for copies of this pamphlet, I feel that I must again take the field for the people that I love, for justice, yea, for common humanity.

May the righteous Judge, who knows how utterly sick my soul is of the awful brutalities perpetrated in this Christian (?) land against an inoffensive, industrious, sober people, inspire my thought and guide my hand to show the hideousness of such crimes, and their sure penalty! May what I write not only free me as *a Christian* from the responsibility and penalty of silence before wrong, but also move some stronger, more eloquent voice to cry for justice and righteousness in the land!

To those who desire to inform themselves further on the Chinese question, I commend Rev. Dr. Gibson's reliable book, "The Chinese in America" (publishers, Cranston & Stowe, Cincinnati, O.), and Hon. George F. Seward's very excellent, just and exhaustive work, "Chinese Immigration in its Social and Economical Aspects" (publishers, Charles Scribner's Sons, New York City).

Mr. Seward was our Consul-General at Shanghai, and afterward our Minister to Peking, for several years. His personal knowledge and experience in China, his ability and fair-minded consideration of a subject of which he is so capable of judging, make his book entirely reliable and very valuable.

ESTHER E. BALDWIN.

85 LEXINGTON STREET, EAST BOSTON, MASS.,
Jan. 9, 1886.

PREFACE TO THE THIRD EDITION.

AGAIN, with increasing humiliation for the necessity, I re-issue this pamphlet, with added pages of disgraceful history made by our National Government since the first issue in 1881. I feel that it is criminal for Christian people to remain silent, while oppression and bitter wrong stalk forth from our Congressional Halls. We are told that $500,000 have been subscribed, and as much more will be added if necessary, to circulate anti-Chinese literature, and affect *political* action. I appeal to Christian men—voters—whether it is not time for the American Christian sentiment of this country to have some weight with the Government in Washington. Is it safe for us personally, as Christians, or as a Christian Government—safe for our own interests for time and eternity—to go farther in heaping insult after insult upon a friendly nation that has never wronged us, and thus make possible and safe, oppression, robbery and murder here, and imperil every interest of every Christian Church in the great Empire of China? It behooves us to stop and think, and to remember that the men to whom the voters of this land hand over our government, and the enactment of law, are the *representatives* of said voters and doing *their* work. In the two previous issues of this pamphlet I have, at personal sacrifice, met the expense myself. Unable to do it at this time, the Chinese Sunday Schools, with their teachers and friends, have kindly contributed the amount for the present issue. I herewith desire to acknowledge, with thanks, this generous help, and to express my earnest hope and prayer that this effort may contribute not only toward creating an effective sentiment against further wickedly discriminating laws, but also toward forcing the repeal of *every* such law against the Chinese, and helping to place them as they should be, on just the same footing in this country as all other foreigners—just as fully protected in their "right to life, liberty and the pursuit of happiness."

ESTHER E. BALDWIN.

1218 PACIFIC STREET, BROOKLYN,
April 22, 1890.

MUST THE CHINESE GO?

"The people of the land have used oppression, and exercised robbery, and have vexed the poor and needy; yea, they have oppressed the stranger wrongfully."—EZEK. xxii. 29.

"Therefore all things whatsoever ye would that men should do to you, do ye even so to them."—MATT. vii. 12.

"What you do not like when done to yourself, do not do to others."—CONFUCIUS' *Doctrine of the Mean* (chap. xiii).

THE spectacle now presented by the Government of this country, in its attitude toward the Chinese, even leaving Christianity entirely out of the question, ought to bring the blush of shame to the face of every honorable, fair-minded man. Seeking, even insisting upon, a treaty of amity and trade with a *weaker* people, pledging its national honor for the protection of any of that people who come to us, and yet, knowingly and willfully, allowing for years the most constant, systematic persecution of the Chinese in our land, in defiance of treaty, law, and justice; and finally, at the bidding of the lowest, wickedest, most brutal, of our population,—"the balance of power,"—enacting laws that deliberately insult this very nation with which we have such treaty, violate the whole spirit of our Constitution, dishonor God, and make possible such crimes as the Wyoming massacre.

I believe before God that the anti-Chinese laws, and those who enacted them, are largely responsible for these massacres and other outrages that have made so black a page in our national history the last few years. These laws were a concession to that element in this land which is the most to be feared, and should be the most carefully watched and firmly resisted. Every concession made to it only strengthens and makes said element more domineering and dangerous to the natives of this land.

An Irish washer-woman, who had manifested much indignation that I had *presumed* to bring home with me a Chinese servant, said, "*We* have a right here, *they* haven't." Two months later, an Irish gentleman (?), who showed the same spirit toward our faithful, polite, Christian servant, used the following expressive language: "*We* have a right here that those who are here by the *mere accident of birth* have not." American-born citizens, how do you like such doctrine?

Now, let us consider the charges against the Chinese people that are said to justify the anti-Chinese laws. Here I may as well say that I am prepared to prove the statements I make.

First, "They come here as sort of slaves." This is wholly untrue. They come here as voluntarily as do the immigrants from across the Atlantic. A needy family has heard of "King Sang" ("the Golden Hill"), as they call California; and all the family unite in saving their meagre earnings to send one of their number to this far-famed "Golden Hill," with the hope that he will return able to make life more comfortable for them all.

Some of them came here by *invitation* to build our railroad, which has opened up the great West, and enriched multitudes of men. Others came by like invitation to work in and redeem untillable lands in the West, making millions of acres productive, thus enriching the country.

They did their work faithfully to the end, and have left that much at least of permanent benefit to us. But, asks one, "Are they not in a sense owned, and bound to obey, the six Chinese companies?" Not at all. These companies are simply benevolent and protective societies, such as are common in China, and much to be commended. The Ningpo men in Foochow, for business purposes, form a Ningpo guild; and the Canton men in Shanghai form a Canton guild. There are "six companies" to represent the six districts or counties of the Canton Province, from which come nearly all of the Chinese in the United States. The object of these guilds is to help each other in a friendly way, to relieve any member of the guild in need, to care for them if sick, etc. They all agree to certain rules by which they shall be governed; but the whole thing is entirely voluntary. Any one is at liberty to enter and to withdraw. They are in no sense secret societies or immigration bureaus. Such guilds existed in China long before we were a nation, and are by no means peculiar to the Chinese in the United States.

Second, " *They are of the lowest classes.*" They are of *exactly* the same class as the immigrant from other lands. The *needy poor*, with few exceptions, must ever be the immigrant class. Those who come to us across the Pacific are largely from the respectable farming-class, who fall into laundry-work, shoe-making, etc., because these branches of industry are chiefly open to them. Not one in a hundred of these workers were laundrymen in their own country, but crowded out of every other industry, the large majority took patiently what was left, and they are abused and threatened for even doing that, by such as the so-called " *American* Laundrymen's Association." A fine Christian Chinese gentleman, educated in Mr. Moody's school at Northfield, and a rare Bible scholar, as well as a capable business man, said to a friend of mine in Springfield, Mass.: "Is there nothing they will let me do in this country but wash clothes?" If they desired real estate to farm, I think they would find no little difficulty in purchasing. I have no fear of the Chinese immigrants suffering in comparison with those who come across the Atlantic. It is not the Chinaman who is too lazy to work, and goes to the almshouse or jail. It is not he who reels through our streets, defies our sabbath laws, deluges our country with beer, and opposes all work for temperance and the salvation of our sons from the liquor curse. It is not the man from across the Pacific who commits the fearful crimes we read of in our daily papers, and who is longing to put his hand to our political wheel and rule the United States.

Two intelligent, wealthy business-men of the State of New York, the one a Republican, the other a Democrat, talking with me on the Chinese question, asked, "Why do you not send us decent immigrants?" In reply, I put the following questions, and received in substance the same replies from both gentlemen:

"Did you ever see a drunken Chinaman?" — "No." — "Did you ever see a noisy, boisterous one on the streets?" —

"No." — "Did you ever see one disturbing others, or lounging at saloons, or gossiping?" — "Never." — "Did you ever
see one on the street who did not seem to have some object
in view, and to be going right toward it?" — "I must con-
fess I never have." — "Has a Chinese tramp ever come to
your door?" — "Never." — "Do you hear of them commit-
ting murder, burglaries, or other crimes against our laws?"
"No." — Will you be so kind as to inform me of any other
immigrant class in regard to which you can reply in the
negative as above, and also what you regard as a 'decent
immigrant'?"

Both gentlemen honestly and frankly admitted that this
was an entirely new view of the question. Both stated that
they had formed their opinions from "newspaper *statements;*" and yet these same intelligent men read their
newspapers with brain alert on every other subject than
this, on which they were ready to accept the most libellous
statements against a friendly nation, whose representatives
were, by their own personal observation, the most inoffensive, law-abiding people of our land. But how fearful is the
responsibility of our press, which, so far from being, as it
should be, the educator and conservator of the morals of the
people, a mighty lever to lift them up to the nobility of true
patriotism, is to-day, in a large degree, only the tool of evil
men, stooping to pander to political prejudice and party in-
trigue, sacrificing right, justice, and even humanity for
votes!

Third, "They will bring leprosy." Then what are our
health officers at San Francisco and on the Pacific mail steamers doing? What our Consul at Hong Kong? What that
important "Commission of Immigration" appointed in 1872
by the California Legislature, and empowered to examine
every one that lands, morally and physically? Dr. Stout, of
the California State Board of Health, in reply to the question whether the Chinese were introducing leprosy, said:
"I think that this hue and cry is simply a farce. It has
come from Europe if it has come at all, and that very
rarely." I declare that this charge is absurd. Lepers are
not numerous in China, and are as a rule separated in their
own villages, and are far more anxious to go out of life than
out of their own country. There are no more healthy immigrants than the Chinese. Invalid Chinese have no desire

to leave their native land. Chinese immigrants sail from a British port, Hong Kong, where it is the duty of the American Consul and English authorities to see that they come voluntarily ; and I take it there is no partiality shown by our authorities to the Pacific Mail Steamship Company over the Atlantic steamship companies, in allowing them to receive immigrants without a clean bill of health. The most decent, neat, healthy, and orderly immigrants I have ever seen and travelled with were the Chinese crossing the Pacific.

The twelve hundred Irish that boarded our steamer at Queenstown were in great contrast to these in many respects. Two were ill when taken aboard, and both died at sea within a few days. Nine hundred immigrants was the legal capacity of the steamer ; yet she took in twelve hundred, and left six hundred more wailing on the shore because they could not come to " blissed free Ameriky."

" *Fourth,* " *China is so crowded that there is great danger of her pouring out her millions and flooding our land.*"

" *Fifth,* " *They do not come to stay, but just to make what they can in a short time, and go back home and take their earnings.*"

I place the fifth beside the fourth, before replying to the latter, just to show how lovely and consistent they look together. If the fourth is dangerous, surely the fifth should encourage our terror-stricken souls at such an irruption. And yet the same man will plead both these arguments, in almost the same breath, against the Chinese.

But let us consider number four : " *The Chinese will come in such numbers as to flood our land.*"

In twenty-five years a hundred and fifty thousand Chinese have come to this country ; that is to say, with all the pressure of their poverty, and all the promise this land has held out to them of successful industry, together with the facilities provided for a speedy and cheap transit hither, in a quarter of a century, *fewer* have come here from China than in a few months of the last year alone from Europe. What curious inequality of mind leads us to fear the flooding by the few, while we open wide the gates to the many ? Again, the Chinese here are almost to a man from the Canton Province ; it is a *local* immigration. The whole nature and education of the Chinese are against removing from one place to another, even in their own country. Only the greatest pressure of circumstances can induce them to leave their native place. Generation after generation of the same family have lived in the same locality. The home of their fathers, the graves of their ancestors, filial piety, every thing that a Chinaman holds dear, gathers around, and binds him to, his native place. It is said that there are only a hundred surnames in all China. The very word for *people* is *pak sang,* "the hundred surnames." A large village often has but two surnames, such as Ting and Tang. To these two families the village belongs, and has belonged for ages; and all their interests are centred there. The sacredness of family ties is nowhere more carefully taught than in China. A cousin of the second degree is called brother, and all family ties imply duties which can not be shirked. The Chinaman, from his earliest days, is taught that his highest duty is to his parents; and upon the condition of obeying, serving, and supporting them in this life, and making sacrifices to their spirits after death, depends his prosperity here and his eternal welfare. This universally recognized duty must ever be a great obstacle to emigration, and the sure pledge of their return to their native land. We may call all this foolish; but I honor the Chinaman for his obedience to his convictions of right, and think many a Christian might learn a much-needed lesson from his zeal. As to the charge that a Chinaman forfeits his citizenship if he is absent from his country beyond a certain time, I answer, that is all nonsense. There is no such law and no such penalty.

And now for charge fifth : " *They do not come to stay, but to make all they can in a short time, and then return home and take all their earnings with them.*"

Intelligent men who know too much to fear a Chinese flood, and who are too just to countenance their persecution, still quote this argument. Let us look at it. Of course it neutralizes and renders harmless No. 4 at once. It is true they do not come to stay ; and I can't help saying, What a pity some others do not follow their example ! Did they do so, I would not have heard this apology from an intelligent man for the corruption of our political parties : "You must remember," said he, "all we have to contend with,—that foreigners control our politics." The problem of a successful republican government, with universal suffrage, has not yet been worked out.

However, there is nothing in our Constitution or laws which defines the length of time any one must promise to stay in this land to secure him the right of entrance. But this objection becomes the veriest mockery, when we remember the *welcome* we give these strangers, and how *comfortable* we make them while here. The mud thrown by Christian boys (of course they are not heathen) upon the snowy clothes ready to iron after the weary washing by the Chinese laundry-man, the broken windows, the stones, the grossest abuse by people and press, the palpable falsehoods against the Chinese published by many of the most respectable papers,—all these *do not* strike one as the wisest arguments a Christian people can use to induce the Chinese to stay. But if this *is* an argument against the Chinaman, what about the American in China? He goes there for the express purpose of making all the money he can, whether it be from tea, silk, or opium; to spend as little as possible in China,—importing his stores and clothing from London, New York, or San Francisco,—and only buying perishable meats, vegetables, and fruit in China; and bringing home with him all his earnings (ten dollars to every one the Chinaman takes out of our country), and I regret to say not always leaving a blessing or an improved people behind him. But the contributions of the Chinese to our wealth as a nation, during all these years of their persecution, grow in value as we look into them. When we wanted to unite the halves of our great continent by rail, in order to develop our resources, the authorities by their own testimony, tried first to do it through the immigrant from across the Atlantic. The sworn testimony of these authorities before a Congressional Committee was that said effort was a failure. If the hour for the men to begin work was 8 A. M., they were just as likely to come at 9 o'clock. Whiskey drinking, fighting, with other evils, and poor irregular work prevailed, and finally in self-defense they sent for Chinese to do the work. They came, and by testimony, not too gladly given, did the work faithfully and well, giving entire satisfaction in *conduct* as well as work. They did like service in other parts of the Pacific coast. They also went cheerfully into thousands of acres of overflowed lands, where no other immigrant would

go because of the exposure, and redeemed those lands for
the use and residence of those, who now turn to kick their
benefactors out of the country! These lands that previously
did not return one penny to the State or any human being,
now produce from 50 to 90 bushels of wheat to the acre.
The Surveyor-General of California declared, that in the two
items alone of railroads and redeemed lands, the Chinese
had enriched California by over $280,000,000. It has been
estimated that of $15,000,000 made by the Chinese annually
in this country $13,000,000 are actually expended here, leav-
ing only $2,000,000 to send home, which is probably con-
siderably more than they do send. But the Chinese are not
the only people who send money out of the country. Before
me is a newspaper paragraph, headed " Remembering their
Friends in the Old Country." I quote it, " The Irish girls in
this country are continually sending financial aid to the
relatives and friends whom they left behind them, and at
this season of the year, the sums sent across the ocean by
the domestics in this city (Boston), are in the aggregate
very large. According to one Boston banker, these remit-
tances this fall have been in excess of any previous year.
During the past four weeks, he alone has made out for servant girls, drafts or bills of exchange amounting to $70,-
000." Chinese send a few hundreds to parent, wife and
child, and the newspaper heading reads " They send all their
money out of the country." I myself heard J. Boyle
O'Reilly, editor of the Boston *Pilot*, a leading Catholic paper, and of course an undisputed authority—declare, in a
lecture on the wrongs of Ireland, that " the Irish question
is not only an *Irish* question, but an *American eco-
nomic* question," for, said he, " the Irish send out of this
country every year to Ireland $70,000,000!!!" The Hon.
Geo. F. Seward, our former Consul-General and Minister to
China, in his valuable book on " Chinese Immigration "
(which I commend to all), shows from official statistics, that
the Chinese in taxes and in work give to California in a
single year the amazing sum of $14,000,000, and this does
not include their large contributions in railroads and redeemed lands. At the very time when the Knights (?) of
Labor rose in Seattle, Washington Territory, to drive out
the Chinese by mob violence, these Chinese were paying far
more taxes than all the " Knights " together, and the city

government was then owing the Chinese merchants $30,000 which it had borrowed from them. O, shame! shame! on such injustice. A few Americans put American steamers on the Yang-tse River, enriched themselves, and ruined thousands of Chinese families, who, with their ancestors, had had the junk-trade of that river for generations; yet these men, suffering under a real wrong, resorted not to an anti-American law, neither to robbery or murder.

Sixth, " They pay no taxes."

This charge is either made through ignorance inexcusable, because the truth is readily to be attained, or through willful falsehood. Several years ago (1876), " the eleven thousand Chinese in San Francisco paid nine thousand dollars in taxes on real estate and personal property; and this in spite of the invidious legislation against them, and the great difficulty of their securing real estate. Every Chinaman paid his two dollars poll-tax,—many of them two and three times the same year," being helpless in the hands of swindlers. "This added ten thousand dollars, making nineteen thousand dollars. To this add twenty-five thousand dollars for licenses, and we have the neat sum of forty-four thousand dollars annual revenue to the city of San Francisco alone." Besides this, the Chinese of that city alone paid the same year internal revenue license five thousand dollars, and stamp tax on cigars made during the year to the enormous sum of three hundred and sixty thousand dollars, or over a thousand dollars each working-day. The grand total of public revenue from the Chinese of San Francisco alone, during 1876, reached the magnificent sum of four hundred and nine thousand dollars. A part of this money was paid for the public-school fund, but no schools were provided for the Chinese. These figures do not include the tax of five dollars (for a time it was fifty dollars) collected from every Chinaman landing in this country, and *from no other immigrant ;* nor hundreds of thousands of dollars collected under the provisions of the Foreign Miners' Tax Law, four dollars a month for every miner, which tax was seldom collected of any others than the Chinese, the law being specially for their benefit. Collector Austin himself informed my friend Dr. Gibson, from whose reliable and able book I collect these statistics, that " there is less difficulty in collecting taxes from the Chinese than from any other class of inhabitants, and less delin-

quencies among them." "But this matter of revenue mul-
tiplies, as we look at it." The imposts or duties on rice
alone brought by the China trade, and mostly consumed by
Chinese, amount to over one million dollars gold coin annually; duty on oil and opium, two hundred and seventy
thousand dollars more; and the duties on other imports
swell the figures to over two million dollars customs collected
annually in the port of San Francisco on the trade from
China, and mostly from Chinamen. Add all this revenue
together, and we have the not insignificant sum of two million, four hundred and nine thousand dollars, including taxes,
licenses, and customs. The Chinese also patronized the in-
surance companies of that city to the amount of over fifty
thousand dollars annually. "Moreover, many of them wear
garments made of our cloth, wear our boots and hats, are fond
of our watches and sewing-machines. They ride in our cars
and steamers. They eat our fish, beef, and potatoes, and in
some parts do much to exhaust the pork market. In this
last item alone, they have paid to producers on the Pacific
coast over a half million of dollars annually." Finally, as
the same author has said so truly, "These croakers about
the Chinese sending all their money home ought to know
that the fortunes amassed by American merchants in China,
and brought to this country, amount every year in the aggregate to five times more than all these Chinamen can
send to China as the fruits of their daily toil."

Seventh, "They do not bring their wives here."

A Chinaman when asked *why* he didn't bring wife and
children here, replied : "It is as much as I can do to keep
my own head on my shoulders here; what could I do with
wife and children also to protect?" American merchants,
naval officers, sea captains and others, go to China and frequently leave their families in this country, but not for any
such reason as the above, as they would be perfectly safe
in China. I and mine were for nearly twenty years.

The customs of most eastern nations seclude women. In
China there is more than this custom to keep the wife at
home. According to the education of the Chinese, it is the
highest duty of the wife to be the keeper at home, and especially to serve the parents of her husband in his absence,
and to attend to the affairs of the family, which she often
does with great skill   It would indeed be an unfilial son who

left his parents without the care of his wife. This may strike the American (in whom filial piety is a virtue fast fading out) as most foolish; but then it is certainly no crime, and no reasonable cause for excluding the Chinese from the United States. This may tend to immorality, but not to the extent practiced by not a few early residents of California, who had families in both the East and West. In the Chinaman's case, the first wife is the chief always. This can not be said of American polygamists. I regret to say that such an argument carried out would speedily terminate the residence of many an American and European in China. It would be as well not to press this argument in the face of Mormonism, and the well-known lives of various people not a thousand miles from anybody. But that this charge may also cease, let me say that the laws dictated by the hoodlum forbid any bringing of Chinese wife or child here. I append my *official* proof, and could duplicate it over and over again.

In the spring of 1887, I received the following statement from a friend in New Haven: "There is a Chinese in this city who has been in our Sunday School about four years. He is very studious, amiable, obliging and faithful. He has made friends not only with the people of the church to which his school belongs, but also with other families of culture, refinement and wealth, and this because of his excellent qualities of mind and heart. Last August he went to China, and he now desires to return here and bring his wife and little son six years old. He appeals to his teachers and friends here to help him to prove his good character, and assist him in securing the admission of his family to this country. Can you tell us the means to be employed to bring this man's wife to America?" This appeal was sent to me as "the Champion of the Chinese." I read it with inexpressible shame, knowing that any American might go to China with his family without let or hindrance. I wrote at once in reply that they should assume, what was the fact—and I was supported in my position by able authority—that the Restriction Act did not include, by letter or spirit, the exclusion of wife or child of any man lawfully here under the treaty. But as I knew that the officers in San Francisco would make trouble in the case, I advised a petition to Secretary Manning of the Treasury, requesting the issuing

of the needful papers, for this wife and son to be admitted
without objection. This petition was sanctioned and signed
by many of the most prominent professors, ministers and
teachers of New Haven. I append only a few of the many
well-known names: ex-Pres. Porter, of Yale; William M.
Barlow, Prof., of Yale; Levi Jois, M.D.; Francis Bacon,
M.D.; James K. Thatcher, Prof. Med. Dep't, Yale; J. H.
Cannolt, Prof., Yale; Rev. Newman Smythe, Pastor First
Cong. Church; M. C. White, M.D., Prof., Yale. I now
give for the benefit of all fair-minded people, and especially
for *voters*, a true copy of the reply received very promptly:

" TREASURY DEPARTMENT, OFFICE OF THE SECRETARY,
       " WASHINGTON, D. C., March 1, 1887.

" MOSES C. WHITE, M. D., AND OTHERS, NEW HAVEN,
   CONN.:

  " *Gentlemen*—The department is in receipt, by reference
from Hon. O. H. Platt, of your communication of the 1st
ultimo, requesting that instructions be issued to the Collector of Customs at San Francisco, to permit the wife and
little son of Mr. Ip-ki-tsak, a Chinese laborer residing at
New Haven, to enter the United States. In reply, you are
informed that, inasmuch as it appears from your statement
that Mrs. Ip-ki-tsak was not in the United States prior to
the expiration of ninety days after the passage of the
Chinese Restriction Act of May 6, 1882, and in view of the
existing decisions of the department, and the U. S. Circuit
Court of California, to the effect that the wife of a Chinese
laborer is a person whose original entry into this country is
prohibited by said act, the department has no power under
the law to grant your request. Respectfully yours,
                        "C. S. FAIRCHILD,
                            " Acting Secretary."

  In consequence of this wresting of both the spirit and letter of the law, whether by decisions of the Treasury Department or United States Courts, Mr. Ip-ki-tsak was compelled to return here without his family. On the steamer in
which he returned came four prostitute Chinese women,
who were promptly landed, no court or department decision
proving the least obstacle! A few weeks later the following telegram from San Francisco appeared in our papers:

"SAN FRANCISCO, Oct. 2.

"The Chinese steamer this week brought over forty-four women, all but four of whom were without the necessary papers. By the usual *habeas corpus* routine these women will doubtless be landed."

As I am accustomed to verify statements before giving them to the public, I immediately returned the telegram to a friend in San Francisco, who is in a position to know the truth, and requested him to write me whether the statement was correct. I quote from his reply : "Your letter to hand. It is a perfectly correct statement which you have sent, with this addition, that they *were all* prostitutes. Cargoes of such women are landed here with or without certificates, while wives of respectable Chinese like Woo-kim Yin, the Methodist merchant here, can not land. The custom officers do good work, but the *courts* throw open the gates. It is maddening to think of the writ of *habeas corpus*, that sacred birth-right of Anglo-Saxons, and the safe-guard of our liberties, being turned into a slave-chain to drag these women down to hell. There could not be landed a single one but for the aid of *American lawyers* and American courts. There are decent and moral Chinese in San Francisco, whom we call heathen, who cry shame on us for practices which are not so much as thought of in their country."

The writer of the above has lived a number of years in China, as well as in San Francisco, and knows whereof he speaks. I ask in all fairness, in view of the above facts, if anything more ought to be said against the Chinese for not bringing their families here. Our graceful attitude is that of silence and humiliation.

Eighth, "They are opium smokers, and are teaching Americans its use." Americans are by no means dependent upon foreign teachers for such instruction. But in view of the great European and American firms in China, which for years have dealt out opium to the Chinese by the *wholesale*, the less we say on this subject the better. This point pressed would prove fatal to many an American and European in China, would indeed prove almost a "restriction act." How did opium go into China? The Chinese Government had national prohibition of opium, save only for medical purposes, and punished with the utmost severity any of its people who violated this law. One hundred years ago no such vice existed in China. About that time the Portuguese, seeing an opportunity to gratify their greed, commenced to smuggle opium into China. The great East India Company, then in control of India, at once proceeded to profit by the example of the unprincipled Portuguese, and also took up the smuggling of opium, only on a far more extended scale; and this in spite of the protests of the Chinese Government. When refused entrance to the port of Canton, they established *heavily armed* receiving ships at the island of Lin Tin, at the mouth of the Canton River—and from there ran boats, also armed, and loaded with the contraband opium, into Canton under cover of night. This was done for sixty years. Finally the Chinese Government sent Commissioner Lin from Peking to Canton with full authority to arrest and punish offenders, and to seize and destroy the opium. He did his work nobly and well, shut up the American and English merchants in their factories, seized $2,500,000 worth of opium, dug pits in the earth, put the opium in them, filled them with water, and floated said drug out to sea. What was the result? Did Christian England applaud? Did the United States cry well done? Nay, verily? England promptly sent her ships of war, with soldiers, cannon and swords, and deliberately went to war with China, and, because might was stronger than right, conquered, and compelled China to pay $21,000,000—$12,000,000 for the war, $3,000,000 to English merchants for property which they professed had been injured, and $6,000,000 for the $2,500,000 worth of opium destroyed; and in addition forced the cession to England of her beautiful Island of Hong Kong, and also compelled the opening of the five Treaty Ports to trade. That I may not be charged with misstating facts as to the occasion of this war, I quote Mr. Gladstone's words uttered in Parliament. He declared: "A war more unjust in its origin, a war more calculated to cover this country with permanent disgrace, I do not know, and have not read of." Again, in the same speech, he said: "They gave you notice to abandon your contraband trade; when they found that you would not, they had a right to drive you from their coasts, on account of your obstinacy in persisting in this infamous and atrocious traffic." Whom did Mr. Gladstone address in these severe words? The English Government, for that

Government had not only defended the East India Company in its violations of the Chinese laws, but had actually taken the whole traffic out of the hands of that company, and for years itself engaged in this illicit traffic. After the war it tried, through its Commissioner, to induce that grand old Emperor, *Tau Kwang*, to legalize the traffic in opium. That so-called Christian Commissioner exhausted every argument, finally urging that by a *"high license"* a large revenue might be secured to the Chinese Treasury. But the grand old man stoutly resisted. Would that his final reply might reach the ears and hearts of at least all Christian voters in this land: *" I will never reap a revenue from the weakness and misery of my people."* English soldiers behind English guns forced this hero to pay $21,000,000, and to cede a part of his vast Empire to a robber government. But neither guns nor might could conquer that invincible spirit, and so that cowardly government proceeded to violate law and bring opium into China without permission, until another war was the consequence, and this time the young Emperor who had succeeded Tau Kwang was unable to resist great England's might, and was compelled to sign the document legalizing the ruin of millions of souls. As he did so, the tears rolled down his cheeks as he exclaimed: "I do this, I know, for the ruin of my people, but can not help myself." And from that day to this England has forced this infamous traffic upon China, as her own minister declared, "against the conscience of the whole people." Our own American merchants' hands are black with the traffic, as are those of almost every other foreign merchant in China. These merchants are not in a few small "opium joints," such as are made so much of here by the anti-Chinese element, but in great wholesale establishments, dealing it out for the ruin of the people by the chest, *Christian* (?) merchants from all the chief Christian nations of the earth have been and are in this traffic: the English Government forcing the Indian farmers to plant the poppy on the fair plains of India, and selling the opium to merchants to poison China. Understand, my dear reader, this opium business is an *English* Government *monopoly*. The merchants buy it from the Government.

This cursed traffic has indeed wrought ruin enough to justify the rallying cry of a mob when, years ago, driving for-

eigners out of their city, they cried after them : "You
killed our Emperor, you burned our summer palace, you are
poisoning our people, you are devils !" Some of us who
know the truth, and the bitter, bitter wrong, cry out:
"How long, O Lord, how long?" We grow impatient for
the Divine arm of retribution to be stretched out in redress
of the oppressed. If a little of this opium filters through
into the United States and a great deal of it into England,
let us make no word of complaint, for the few Chinese in the
traffic here are only following afar off, and in a very small
way, the distinguished example of renowned American and
English merchants. I close my answer to the opium charge
with a financial and moral question so simple that the
primary school child can understand it. China's opium bill
for her 400,000,000 of people is about $75,000,000. The
United States' liquor bill for its 60,000,000 of people is
$900,000,000. Which is the larger? which is the worst?
Shall we point our finger at the "mote" in our brother's
eye, driven there by the weight of a Christian nation, while
we deliberately choose, vote to have, a "beam" in our own
eye?

*Ninth, " They endanger our morals, especially by their
evil women."*

If the Great Judge of all the earth, sitting on his throne
of justice and righteousness, ever laughs in derision at
wrong, methinks he does when the anti-Chinese party, with
all their record, dare to talk of injury to *their* morals.

I fell in with one of their most lusty champions on a train.
He declared himself to be an infidel, his wife the same ; be-
lieved in lynch-law, especially for the Chinese, his only
charge against them being that they find work in this land ;
told, with fiendish delight, of his share in " cleaning out one
of their camps." Said he, " Do you know that man Gibson?" (the late Rev. Dr. Gibson, the heroic superintendent
of Methodist mission-work among the Chinese on the Pacific
coast). I replied, " Yes; he is a dear personal friend of
ours, who worked nobly in our mission for ten years,"—
" Ah, *we hate* him ! We'd like to have his heart." Such
were the brutal words of this man, outwardly a gentleman,
but betrayed, under the intense excitement of his hatred of
the Chinese, to reveal the foul, murderous nature within.
And yet *he* could talk of morals. Does it not become a bur-

lesque when such men fear for morality ? I could but think that if the respectable gentleman I have met, who have sympathy with this anti-Chinese element, could have seen and heard this "shining light," they would have been heartily sick of such association.

And will the Californians use this plea for protection to *their* morals ?

The horrors that I heard, and facts that polluted the air, in San Francisco and smaller towns, come up to me so vividly, that I am amazed that people living in *so frail a* "*glass house*" dare to throw a stone like this at the more respectable house of the Chinese. There are many good people in California, and I honor them for their struggle against wrong. But, alas ! the reputation of San Francisco and other places is badly tattered. I shall never forget the shock I experienced, when, just after our arrival in San Francisco from China, we were on our way to church one *Sunday* morning, and a man went shouting through the street, "Sweet oranges, fresh peas for sale !" and our Chinese servant quietly remarked, "Teacheress, it is just about the same here as in China, isn't it?" I then awakened to the realization of the fact that I was in a Christian city where the Sabbath was not regarded. But to return to the Chinese women. So far as I have seen, they are at least decently *clothed*, which is more than I can say of the white creatures of the same class I saw in San Francisco. There is also this difference. The latter have *chosen* their life of sin in the full blaze of the saving Christian light of this land ; while the Chinese woman in San Francisco has probably had no choice in her life, and certainly *no light* from Christianity. She is, in a large majority of cases, more sinned against than sinning.

But let the pleader of this last refuge of lies tread carefully here, and note the following :—

"In 1872 the Legislature of California passed a law creating a commissioner of immigration, with power to examine immigrants, and to forbid the landing of those whom he should find to be criminals, or lewd persons, or afflicted with contagious diseases. Under the provisions of that Act, the commissioner forbade the landing of twenty-five Chinese women from the steamer 'Japan,' which arrived in August, 1873. The women-dealers, by the help of lawyers of a cer-

tain class, obtained a writ of *habeas corpus*, and brought
the women on shore before Judge Morrison of the Fourth
District Court. The judge sustained the commissioner, and
remanded the women back to the steamship company to be
returned to China.

"Immediately after Judge Morrison's decision was pronounced, Messrs. Edgerton & Quint obtained a writ of
habeas corpus from Chief Justice Wallace of the Supreme
Court, upon the allegation that the women were illegally de-
tained by the captain of the 'Japan.' The writ was execu-
ted, and the women escorted back to the county jail."

The Supreme Court of the State of California sustained
the ruling of Judge Morrison, and the women were a second
time remanded back to the steamer. But the women-dealers
and their unprincipled lawyers then applied to the United
States District Court, procured a third writ *habeas corpus*,
and the case was tried before that tribunal, which *reversed*
the decision of Judge Morrison and the Supreme Court of
California, pronounced the law under which the commissioner had acted unconstitutional, and ordered the women to
be allowed their freedom. Respectable Chinese merchants
in San Francisco stood ready to pay the passage of such
women right back to China. The Chinese Government itself (without doubt) would quickly respond to any action on
the part of our Government for excluding Chinese vice;
though it might in fairness insist upon a speedy clearing of
its own ports of like women, gamblers, and drunkards, *not*
Chinese. We have been forced to endure the company of
such white women (Americans) on our way to China, and
have felt that the less we said about our national morality,
the better. *Any* and *all evils* found to-day in Chinatown,
San Francisco, are simply a *shame* to the authorities of that
city, and *entirely* under their control. There are no people
more amenable to law than the Chinese.

But, alas! it is by no means a secret that the very officers,
who, in San Francisco, by solemn oath are bound to do their
utmost to stop crime, wink at it for the sake of the bribes
with which their hands are black. Evil men come from
China as from other countries; but the bad Chinaman can
be sent back, or controlled more easily than others. Chinese gambling-dens and brothels can be utterly rooted out
of Chinatown whenever the high-minded officers of that

city can consent to forego the bribes they now receive. When they have attained to so high a state of grace as this, and Chinatown is cleaned up, I would humbly suggest that, if they put on their glasses and look around, they may find a few other like dens not imported from China; and similar places may be found in Philadelphia, New York, Brooklyn, and the model city of Boston itself, to say nothing of the moral (?) cities of Chicago and Cincinnati. "Consistency, thou *art* a jewel!"

In the mean while, let the American people meditate upon the answer of the president of one of the "Six Chinese Companies," in San Francisco, to Mayor Bryant, in reply to his condemnation of Chinese prostitution. "Yes, yes, Chinese prostitution *is* bad. What do you think of German, French, Spanish, and American prostitution? Do you think them good?" This astute heathen wondered at the Christian (save the mark!) silence and forebearance toward the *many*, and the loud *horror-stricken* hoot at the few. Very stupid and heathenish the question, no doubt; but then we *can't* make a law to prevent the Chinese from thinking, questioning, and drawing conclusions. But what of the morality of many of the American merchants, naval officers and captains and others in China, and I might add in India, Japan, and all other places to which our commerce goes? Would that, in justice to imperiled human souls, I might maintain my usual silence here! But I dare not. The enemy is mighty —we are a weak folk—and I must, as before God, meet every charge, and prove at least that we should not demand more of these Eastern people, who never heard of the decalogue, than we do of those born and bred under its commands. How are our college-bred, Christian-born men living in the East? Alas! that I must say it of the majority of them, in such a way as would bring grief and shame to every Christian parent, wife and child at home. Glad am I to say that there are noble exceptions, but the rule remains. God forgive them for so shaming us before the heathen, and for putting by far the greatest obstacle in the way of our missionary work that we ever meet. Imagine the chagrin and humiliation of my husband, with other missionaries, when, as was so customary, in preaching to an audience of natives, after telling them of the great one God, His work in creation, the fall of man and our hope in Christ, he proceeds to expound man's duty toward that creator, as given in the first table of the law, the brotherhood of man, and man's duty to his brother as taught in the second table, a keen, courteous man in his audience, rises and in most respectful word and manner asks, "Teacher, may I say a word?" The "Teacher" can only assent, for there the pew may reply to the pulpit. The "heathen" proceeds to say: "Teacher, what you have said is good. The native people believe that all men are brothers—and that we should be kind and just to all. You need not have crossed thousands of miles of ocean and left your honorable country and venerable parents to come to tell us this, for our teacher Confucius told us this hundreds of years ago. We believe it; but, to give me to see, your people don't believe these doctrines which you teach. You say, 'Keep sacred the worship (Sabbath) day.' We know nothing of this worship day—but if it is important, why don't your own people keep it? Don't you know that your merchants are loading their ships with tea to-day as on any other day? You say that the command of your great teacher not to kill, means also not to injure any one. Who brought the opium here? Who forced it upon our Government and people? Who are selling it to our poor people to-day in this place? Isn't it your Jesus doctrine people? You say that another of your Teacher's commands is to be pure in life. Surely, teacher, you know how your men are living here, just across the river in your foreign settlement! Are they clean?" Alas! alas! that this is no fancy sketch, but a true description of what has occurred. To my most bitter knowledge the great and all important fact that there is one true God and Saviour Jesus Christ was often rendered ineffectual, by the ever present, evil example of those who were justly supposed to be His followers; for as it is customary here to term all those Eastern people heathen—so do they suppose us all to be Christian. "*First*, cast out the *beam* out of thine own eye; and then shalt thou see clearly to cast out the mote out of *thy brother's* eye."

Tenth, "*The Chinese cheapen labor, and throw others out of employ.*" The cry not so many years ago in California was against the exorbitant prices demanded for labor. A few had command of the labor market, making many lucrative industries impossible by their high demands. To-day it is against the cheap labor of the Chinese, but this argument is reserved for strangers who are ignorant of Western prices.

There is absolutely no such thing as cheap labor on the Pacific Coast. An untrained Chinaman commands from three to five dollars a week, and board, in kitchen employ; Chinese cooks, from twenty to forty dollars a month, and board. Is this cheap labor? A gentleman from the Pacific Coast, whom I met in Rome, made to me, as one of his charges against the Chinese, this one of "cheap labor," but quickly yielded the point when he found that I was posted on prices in California. *The Chinaman takes the place of no one who will do the work as well as he;* but when unfaithfulness, dishonesty, and utter disregard of the employer's interests are superseded by faithfulness, honesty, and a recognition of duty to give a fair return in work for wages received, who will complain of such a change?

Eleventh, "The Chinaman wears a cue, retains his own style of dress, and eats rats and puppies."

There is so much bigotry and ignorance in these complaints, that they are almost unworthy of notice; yet, as they are really given as grounds of complaint, I notice them.

The "Father of his Country" wore a cue. Many of our young ladies to-day do the same. The Chinaman's cue is a badge of his loyalty to his Government, and as such he has no right to dispense with it; neither is it any of our business how he dresses his hair. He has likewise the same natural right to retain his own dress: the foreigners in China do the same. I and mine arrayed ourselves, and dressed our hair, in China after our own style; and no Chinaman was discourteous or *impertinent* enough to find fault with us.

The rat and dog eating charge is simply disgraceful, and those who make it only illuminate their ignorance before the public. In nearly twenty years' residence in China, and visiting different parts of the country, I never saw or heard of such a thing but once, when a poor low-class man was charged with partaking of dog-meat; and it excited as much indignation among his associates as it would have done here. I have heard that in exceptional poverty-stricken cases, such food has been taken, and that it is sold in some restaurants at Canton; but to state, as some of our school-books do, that the Chinese eat rats and dogs, and enforce the libel by

that ancient and disgraceful picture of a Chinaman with a
bamboo across his shoulder, with dogs at one end, and rats
at the other, thereby conveying the impression that such
is the general diet of the Chinese, is to slander the people
of China. It would be just as true for a Chinaman to visit
the United States and England, and go home and state to
his people that Americans eat frogs, and Englishmen horse-
meat. I, for one, protest against any such public-school
teaching to my children.

*Twelfth, " They look so impassive, keep themselves to
themselves as though they had no hearts."*

Well, it is amazing that they don't run into our arms !
We could aim our *stones* more surely then, and the *mud*
would spatter more generally !   " Love your enemies,"
"pray for them who curse you," are *Christian* teachings,
that, alas! the "heathen Chinee" has never learned. He
has learned the lesson *not* to strike back *well* in this land.

The Chinaman's idea of courtesy will forever prevent his
pressing his company upon us as "a stranger guest" among
us; but there are many in this land who can testify to his
quick and grateful response to the slightest kindness. Their
gratitude to, and appreciation of, their Sunday-school teachers in Boston, New York, Brooklyn, and every other place
where they have such attention, is constantly shown in the
most practical, beautiful, and generous manner. Grand,
true, Christian workers will testify to the truth of this asser-
tion. In this connection I desire to quote the telling words
of a lady resident in Connecticut, who speaks out my sentiments :

" It is seventeen years to-day since my brother, a young
man of rare promise, laid down his life on a Southern battle-
field in defence of human rights; and his blood cries out
against those who are trying to make us believe that God
and our fathers meant only black and white men when they
declared the nations of one blood. Ten years ago we received
into our household two Chinese lads, twelve years of age,
who came from the middle, or merchant, class, and were
members of the Chinese Educational Mission recently re-
called. These boys, taken from heathen surroundings, were
not only as intelligent, courteous, and refined as any youths
in this Christian land, but they were exceptionally noble and
high-minded. During all these years they have grown into

the heart of our family life, tender of our sick and aged, sorrowing with us over our dead, until they have become our own kindred; and the hopes and ambitions buried in our brother's grave blossom anew, as they live over his experiences in their college career. You can understand, then, how our hearts grow hot with indignation as we hear men, who are not worthy to stand in their presence, speak of our beloved brethren as belonging to an essentially and irreclaimably inferior race. Like the Jews of old, who despised the Gentiles, these noble senators will, some of them, see the despised Chinaman sitting with Abraham and Isaac, and themselves, the children of the kingdom, cast out."

Thirteenth, " The Chinese will not become citizens."

When living in another city of this country, after I had written a series of articles, taking up in detail this whole Chinese question, in a prominent daily paper of that city, and had frequently spoken in public upon the same subject, I learned that such work on my part was exceedingly obnoxious to various labor unions, to the "Knights of Labor" among the rest. Vile, abusive and libelous letters were sent me, and all of them save two, which professed to be from *women*, were anonymous, as were the most of the attacks in the labor union papers. I could not help feeling, that if the Christian people and ministers, some with "D.D." attachments, who have taken their stand in support and defense of this wicked anti-Chinese work, could have seen these letters, they would be ashamed of such company. Finally the Chairman of an Executive Committee of the "Knights of Labor" of that city came and had an interview with me. He told me that they had discussed my work for the Chinese for several hours in their union. I asked him for his charges against the Chinese. He gave them, and I answered them one by one, he declared, to his entire satisfaction. Finally, he said : "I am glad to have had this talk with you, I shall never think, as I did, of you and your work; but there is still one more charge, and it is the chief with us laboring men, which you can not answer ;—They will not become citizens!" I replied, "Would you put out a man's eyes, and then abuse him for not seeing?" He asked, "What do you mean?" "I mean that we have a national law that the Chinese shall never become citizens?" He sprang to his feet in great excitement, and insisted that there was *no* such law, *could* not

be, adding " Why that is our chief charge against them !"
I as firmly and emphatically assured him that there existed
at that moment said law, and also assured him that I was
well aware that probably eight out of ten voters did not
know it—our Government doing an immense amount of
dirty work, that the people did not and could not know, of
slipping bills through under cover of disguised titles and at
the bidding of hoodlums and Jesuits. " Do you mean to say
that you have seen this law in black and white?" he asked.
"I have that law in the house now, and will send you a copy
of it to-morrow morning," I replied. He answered, "I have
not a word more to say; I go to throw a bomb into our
union !" Men, like this man, go on making this charge
against the Chinese; and the hoodlums and that *secret*
power, *that plans* this work and so much else of evil in this
land—gloats over the ignorance of the native voter. I here-
with quote from the Constitution of the State of California,
adopted March 3d, 1879, and submitted to a vote of the people May 7th, 1879. I can not resist the inclination first to
quote from Article I., Section 1, the following :

" All men are by nature free and independent, and have
certain inalienable rights, among which are those of enjoy-
ing and defending life and liberty; acquiring, possessing,
and protecting property, and pursuing and obtaining safety
and happiness." In the very next Article we have the following burlesque upon the above :

"Article II. Right of Suffrage. Section 1. Every native
male citizen of the United States, every male person who
shall have acquired the rights of citizenship under or by
virtue of the treaty of Queretaro, and every male natural-
ized citizen thereof, who shall have become such ninety days
prior to any election, of the age of twenty-one years, who shall
have been a resident of the State one year next preceding
the election, and of the county in which he claims his vote
ninety days, and in the election precinct thirty days, shall
be entitled to vote at all elections, which are now or may hereafter be authorized by law ; *provided,* no native of China,
no idiot, insane person, or person convicted of any infamous
crime, and no person hereafter convicted of the embezzle-
ment or misappropriation of public money, shall ever exercise the privilege of an elector in this State." This villainy
was perpetrated in 1879. Not content with thus honoring

her own State, California, through her rulers, demanded such a law for all the States; and in 1882 their demand was granted, in another discriminating Act against the Chinese, entitled "To execute certain Treaty stipulations relating to the Chinese," passed by the Senate, March 9, 1882. Section 16 reads as follows: "That hereafter no State Court or Court of the United States shall admit Chinese to citizenship; and all laws in conflict with this Act are hereby repealed." Surely this charge may well vanish with the troop that have gone before! But suppose there was no such law, and still the Chinese were so irresponsive to the wonderful liberty and gracious, kindly treatment they receive at our hands, that they did not all hasten to become citizens and vote "early and often," and, like some other foreign guests in this land, only bide their time to seize the whole machinery of our Government; suppose they are so utterly stupid, what right have we to complain? My husband did not go to China to repudiate his loyalty to his own Government and become a subject of the Chinese Emperor; no more do any of our merchants; and we women not being citizens of *any* country, save only from the dim reflected citizenship of our husbands—if we are so fortunate as to have any, we of course never dreamed of being Chinese citizens; and up to date there has never been a Chinese idiotic enough to suggest such an impertinence to the American in China. Consistency, thou art indeed a jewel as rare as beautiful!

And now I have conscientiously and fairly I think,—warmly, with a righteous indignation, I admit,—answered the popular charges against the Chinese. Some one is ready to ask, "If all you have said is true, what is the source of this anti-Chinese howl?" Your question is easily answered.

The Chinese laborers belong to none of the labor unions of this land; worse still, they are the exceptional class that does not patronize the rum-shops. Think of the host of enemies they at once array against them in this last respect, and of the mighty money power in the hands of these foes. Again, they have no vote, and so are worse than worthless to the average politician. *Lastly*, and fatally for the native American, the immigrant from across the Atlantic *desires* and *intends* to command the labor market here; not only to rule in our homes, but in every other department of industry into which he enters; to fix prices of labor, to strike

for more, to do or not to do, without fear of competition.
An efficient competitor is his only obstacle; and that he has
in the patient, faithful, sober, Chinaman. This Atlantic immigrant now holds *the balance of power* at the polls, and
says to the politician, "My competitor who stands in the
way of my inalienable right to rule *must* go;" and down
goes the politician on his knees before the balance of power.
There are a few noble exceptions of *statesmen* who do not
bite the dust in this manner. Such are Senators Hoar,
Dawes, Hawley, Platt, and Wilson, who have stood nobly
for ancient principles and the right; and such too are
there on the Pacific coast, grand men and women who have
held on to justice and right amid an overwhelming and de-
moralizing public opinion.

In speaking of the immigrants from across the Atlantic, I
except the good men and women who are honest, industrious, and sober, and who are in consequence a strength to
our country. I want further to say that there are good men
in the East who really believe the miserable lies concocted
in the West against the Chinese; but I can not regard even
such as excusable. Certainly in these days of intelligence
and facilities for obtaining information, some near approach
to truth could be reached, and should be, before men vote
to exclude a race from the rights granted freely to others.
But, unfortunately, I find that men who read newspaper
statements on other subjects with eyes open and brains alert
just swallow without questioning any thing and every thing
said against the Chinese; *vide* the popular newspaper paragraph that the Chinese Government had beheaded a Chinese
student *in Hong Kong* for falling in love with an American
girl! If the reader and editor did not know that the Chinese Government does not punish its subjects for being
smitten with the charms of the foreign fair one, they at
least ought to have known that Hong Kong is an English
colony, and that the Chinese Government does not behead
its love-stricken subjects under the shadow of the British flag!
And yet this paragraph has been quoted to me against the
Chinese by men of great intelligence. If the Chinese people
are what the American fancy paints them, then the conun-
drum remains how a beneficent Creator could permit *one-
third* of humanity to be of this "vile race." But knowing
them as I do, not from newspaper items and the hatred of

the "balance of power," but from a personal knowledge of all classes of the people in their own country; knowing them to be *industrious* beyond any other people, patient under trial, cheerful under burdens, fond of learning to such an extent that they have a literary instead of a moneyed aristocracy, showing a respect to age almost unknown in this land, filial piety the central virtue around which all others cluster, and upon which their present and eternal welfare hangs, *the* virtue which ever takes them back to their native land and the graves of their fathers,—*knowing* all these to be the marked characteristics of the great Chinese people, I no longer wonder that the Creator has made one-third of the human race after the Chinese pattern, and less than seventy million Americans. Nor do I wonder that he has given to them a country greater in extent than our own, and as rich in minerals, soil, and scenery. I only wonder that he has given to us (who in more respects than one are not the equals of the Chinese) the crowning blessing of humanity,—a knowledge of Christ,—instead of giving it to the greater people. Let us see to it that in our treatment of that people we offend not the King of kings. He may bear long, but in the end we shall certainly reap what we sow, as a nation as well as individuals.

Passing from China to India, on our way we stopped at Singapore and Penang, and were assured there that the men of business integrity, wealth, and good character were the Chinese; and in Calcutta we received no contrary testimony. Time and time again our own American merchants in China have assured me that their Chinese customers were just as reliable as European or American. Our own real-estate agents, customs officials, and tax collectors acknowledge that none in the land are more prompt in the payment of their dues, or more quiet, orderly tenants.

The Mayor of New Orleans lately averred in public that "No more industrious, honest and law-abiding people help to make up the mixed population of New Orleans, than the Chinese."

I here *assert*, fearless of any counter statement *capable of proof*, that the Chinese to-day are the most industrious, quiet, honest, sober, patient, and forbearing (oh, how forbearing!) immigrants in this land. And how have they been treated? If they go into the streets, they are insulted;

if they stay at home, they are not exempt. Newspapers vie with each other in libelling them; even Christian men, through party rule, unite with hoodlums in the cry " Away with them!" They have been compelled to pay their taxes over and over again; are taxed for our schools, and not allowed to attend them. They have been beaten and killed, and no one has redressed their wrongs; nay, more, officers whose business it was to protect have stood by and said, " It is only a Chinaman!"

I must say, with shame and confusion of face, that the heathen Government of China has kept its treaty in our protection in China, and redressed any wrongs we had; while the Christian Government of this land has not even tried to keep its most solemn treaty obligations with China. Chinese have been taxed when entering the country, and when leaving it; invidious taxation in many ways has been put upon them, and laws enacted especially to oppress them; and our Government has interfered in no way for their protection. To show that I make no exaggerated charges, I will give quotations from Western papers, showing how long, and to what an outrageous extent, the crimes against the Chinese have gone. They are mainly from the Rev. Dr. Gibson's valuable book, "The Chinese in America," which I earnestly recommend to those who desire to know the unadulterated truth on this subject. Dr. Gibson was a member of our (Methodist) mission at Foo Chow, China, for ten years. On his return to this land, our missionary board availed itself of his ability and experience by appointing him superintendent of our Chinese mission-work on the Pacific Coast; and bravely for twenty years did he stand in defence of the persecuted Chinese on that coast, often, too, at the peril of his life, even at the cost of the most villainous libels of the anti-Chinese party.

At one of the anti-Chinese meetings, Dr. Gibson was burnt in effigy in the presence of Mayor Bryant, without rebuke; as one paper says, " the mayor looking smiling on!" At one time for weeks, when he left the house, his wife was in anxiety for his life; he received letters threatening his life; and at another time the Mission House had to be protected by police. Again, when on one occasion, he, a free American citizen, was in the California hall of legislation, a member of that honorable (?) body sprang up, and addressing the speaker, shouted, "I move you, sir, that Otis Gibson, the most offensive man to our party on this coast, be expelled the house!" And they actually *dared* to take a a vote on such a proposition, and failed to put him out by only nine votes. He had risen to leave, but sat down to see the result. A few days later, when he was again present, the same outrage was committed. His sole offence in all these years was his Christian work and brave stand in the defence of the Chinese. Dr. Gibson was a hero of the noblest, purest type. His record is made on high, and so is that of his foes and those of the oppressed stranger. Glad am I that there is a righteous Judge, who will with unwavering justice mete out to each according to his deeds.

California has been the breeding-place for anti-Chinese agents. Not content with brutalizing its own people, and disgracing itself, and the rest of our country, before the heathen as well as civilized world, it has sent out its agents along the coast to hawk its lies, and incite to murder and robbery, until "Kearneyites" and "sand-lots" at once suggest their native locality. The Chinese at first were not only welcomed, but invited, to California. The European immigrant demanded four and five dollars a day for work, and every one was helpless before him; but when the Chinaman came, by invitation, he was willing to work for two and three dollars a day. This was his sin at first, and persecution at once commenced; and when prices, by a fair competition, levelled to a somewhat reasonable rate, but by no means to "cheap labor" (for still wages were high compared with those in the East), so that industries formerly impossible could be carried on, enriching the State, this hatred of the Chinese only increased. They had dared to compete, and successfully, with the European laborer, and so were never forgiven. The politician, wanting the votes of those ruling laborers, joined in the cry; and soon official silence, or sanction, made all manner of wrong possible.

The newspaper quotations I now give will fairly hint the state of affairs, but it would take volumes to record the hideous wrongs perpetrated against these helpless strangers in our land. The "Annals of San Francisco," written in 1854, says, "In short, there is a strong feeling—prejudice, it may be—existing in California against all Chinamen, and they are nicknamed, cuffed about, and treated very unceremoniously by every other class; yet they *are generally quiet* and industrious members of society, *charitable among themselves, not* given to intemperance and the rude vices which drink induces."

On this subject "The Nevada Journal" said, "There is a species of semi-legalized robbery perpetrated upon the Chinese. Many of the collectors are gentlemen in every sense of the word, but there are others who take advantage of their position to extort the last dollar from the poverty-stricken Chinese. They date licenses back, exact pay in some instances for extra trouble in hunting up the terrified Chinamen, and by various devices fatten themselves upon the spoils thus obtained. The complaints of the injured and oppressed find no open ear; for is it not declared by the Supreme Court, the highest tribunal of the land, that their oaths are not to be regarded? Under this state of things, the life of a Chinaman in California is one of hardship and oppression." *This is from the extreme West,* please note.

"The North Californian," published in Oroville, delivered the following: —

"As we have once said, so do we now repeat, that we are ready to sanction any honorable measure to prevent our country being overrun with hordes of Asiatics; but we protest against the application of the rack and thumb-screw to the poor, unassuming Mongolians now among us. John Chinaman always has a little money, because he must and will work, whether he earns much or little. He must have cash, or starve, for he can't get trusted for his food; and so he comes down with the dust. In this way, and by means of the *oppressive tax* which he pays for *the privilege of laboring,* he contributes more to sustain trade, and support a government which *refuses* him the *least* protection, than many worse specimens of humanity of a more favored race, who affect to sneer at him as being no better than a brute. Let justice be done, though the heavens fall, and let it be done to John Chinaman."

Such statements from the scene of crime are refreshing and *emphasizing.* Under this system of official and general oppression, of course morals did not improve, and crimes multiplied against the Chinese, until in October, 1876, a congressional joint commission of investigation on the subject of Chinese immigration was held in San Francisco. Sen-

ators Morton of Indiana, Sargent of California, Cooper of
Tennessee, with Representatives Meade of New York, Piper
of California, and Wilson of Iowa, composed the commission.

"It was arranged to have the investigation proceed somewhat after the form of a court-trial; the anti-Chinese party
being the prosecutors, and the Chinese the defendants.
State Senator M'Coppin, Frank M. Pixley, and a certain
Cameron H. King were recognized as the lawyers for the
prosecution. Col. F. A. Bee and B. S. Brooks were attor-
neys for the defence." The following will show Mr. Pixley's
character: "Mr. Pixley made an hour and a half statement of charges against the Chinese, such as, they live
cheaply, are industrious, are not subject to be drafted as
jurymen, do not attend our schools, take no interest in our
politics, etc. He neglected to state that the Chinaman is not
juryman or soldier because we do not allow him to be a citizen, also that he does not attend our schools because the
school boards refuse him admission. He *did* state, however, that *one of the principal dangers to our white laboring population is because the Chinaman labor so well, are
anxious to learn trades, and are quick to acquire knowledge!* On the religious question, Mr. Pixley boldly stated
the view maintained by the prosecution generally, when he
said that he could not speak of the matter of Christianizing
the Chinaman with the gravity which the circumstances
demanded. For his part he did not believe that Chinamen
had souls, or, *if any,* none *worth saving!*"

"Anti-Chinese clubs were organized throughout San
Francisco. The frantic cry was raised, 'Organize, organize?' Politicians organized; loafers, tramps, and bummers
organized. Hoodlum boys of ten and fifteen were encouraged
to join some of these organizations, and have been found
very useful in teaching the Chinese that they are not wanted
in this country."

Excitement finally ran so high, and indignities against
the Chinese so multiplied under the encouragement of officials, that the helpless Chinese were driven to make appeals
for relief. I append one of these, and insist that it is a credit
to the heads and hearts of those persecuted strangers who
prepared it, and that it should bring the utmost shame
and humiliation, not only to every Californian, but as well to

every American voter who has not thrown his influence, as
far as he has any, against the cowardly assaults upon a
helpless people.

A MEMORIAL FROM REPRESENTATIVE CHINA-MEN IN AMERICA.

To His Excellency U. S. Grant,
President of the United States of America.

Sir,—In the absence of any consular representative, we
the undersigned, in the name and in behalf of the Chinese
people now in America, would most respectfully present for
your consideration the following statements regarding the
subject of Chinese immigration to this country :—

First, We understand that it has always been the settled
policy of your honorable Government to welcome immigration to your shores, from all the countries, without let or
hinderance.   The Chinese are not the only people who have
crossed the ocean to seek a residence in this land.

Second, The treaty of amity and peace between the
United States and China makes special mention of the rights
and privileges of Americans in China, and also of the rights
and privileges of Chinese in America.

Third, American steamers, subsidized by your honorable
Government, have visited the ports of China, and invited
our people to come to this country to find employment, and
improve their condition.

Fourth, Our people in this country, for the most part,
have been peaceable, law-abiding, and industrious.   They
performed the largest part of the unskilled labor in the con-
struction of the Central Pacific Railroad, and also of other
railroads on this coast.   They have found useful employment in all the manufacturing establishments of this coast,
in agricultural pursuits, and in family service.   While bene-
fiting themselves with the honest reward of their daily toil,
they have given satisfaction to their employers, and have
left all the results of their industry to enrich the State.
They have not displaced white laborers from these positions,
but have simply multiplied industries.

Fifth, The Chinese have neither attempted nor desired
to interfere with the established order of things in this country, either of politics or religion.   They have opened no

whiskey-saloons for the purpose of dealing out poison, and degrading their fellow-men. They have promptly paid their duties, their taxes, their rents, and their debts.

Sixth, It has often occurred, about the time of the State and general elections, that political agitators have stirred up the mind of the people in hostility to the Chinese; but formerly the hostility has subsided after the elections were over.

Seventh, At the present time an intense excitement and bitter hostility against the Chinese in this land, and against further Chinese immigration, has been created in the minds of the people, led on by his Honor the Mayor of San Francisco and his associates in office, and approved by his Excellency the Governor of the State and other great men of the State. These great men gathered some twenty thousand of people of this city together on the evening of April 5, and adopted an address and resolutions against Chinese immigration. They have since appointed three men (one of whom we understand to be the author of the address and resolutions) to carry that address and those resolutions to your Excellency, and to present further objections, if possible, against the immigration of the Chinese to this country.

Eighth, In this address, numerous charges are made against our people, some of which are highly colored and sensational, and others, having no foundation in fact, are only calculated to mislead honest minds, and create an unjust prejudice against us. We wish most respectfully to call your attention, and through you the attention of Congress, to some of the statements of that remarkable paper, and ask a careful comparison of the statements there made with the facts in the case.

(*a*) It is charged against us, that not one virtuous China-woman has been brought to this country, and that here we have no wives and children.

The fact is, that already a few hundred Chinese families have been brought here. These are all chaste, pure, keepers at home, not known on the public street. There are also among us a few hundred, perhaps a thousand, Chinese children born in America. The reason why so few of our families are brought to this country is because it is contrary to the custom and against the inclination of virtuous Chinese women to go so far from home, and because the frequent

outbursts of popular indignation against our people have
not encouraged us to bring our families with us against
their will.

Quite a number of Chinese prostitutes have been brought
to this country by unprincipled men, but these at first were
brought from China at the instigation and for the gratifica-
tion of white men. And even at the present time it is com-
monly reported that a part of the proceeds of this villainous
traffic goes to enrich a certain class of men belonging to this
honorable nation, a class, too, who are under solemn obliga-
tion to suppress the whole vile business, and who certainly
have it in their power to suppress it if they so desired. A
few years ago, our Chinese merchants tried to send these
prostitutes back to China, and succeeded in getting a large
number on board the steamer; but a certain lawyer of your
honorable nation (said to be the author and bearer of these
resolutions against our people), in the employ of unprincipled Chinamen, procured a writ of *habeas corpus*, and
brought all these women on shore again, and the courts decided that they had a right to stay in the country if they so
desired. These women are still here; and the only remedy
for this evil, and also for the evil of gambling, so far as we
can see, lies in an honest and impartial administration of municipal government in all its details, *even* including the police
department. If officers would refuse bribes, these unprincipled men could no longer purchase immunity from the
punishment of their crimes.

(*b*) It is charged against us, that we have purchased no
real estate. The general tone of public sentiment has not
been such as to encourage us to invest in real estate, and yet
our people have purchased and now own over eight hundred
thousand dollars' worth of real estate in San Francisco
alone.

(*c*) It is charged against us, that we eat rice, fish and
vegetables. It is true that our diet is slightly different from
the people of this honorable country; our tastes in these mat-
ters are not exactly alike, and can not be forced. But is
that a sin on our part of *sufficient gravity* to be brought
before the President and Congress of the United States?

(*d*) It is charged, that the Chinese are no benefit to this
country. Are the railroads built by Chinese labor no benefit to this country? Do not the results of the daily toil of

one hundred thousand men increase the riches of this country?
Are the manufacturing establishments largely worked by
Chinese labor no benefit to this country? Is it no benefit to
this country, that the Chinese annually pay over two million
dollars duties at the custom-house of San Francisco? Is not
the two hundred thousand dollars annual poll-tax paid by
the Chinese any benefit? And are not the hundreds of
thousands of dollars taxes on personal property and the foreign miners' tax, annually paid to the revenues of this country, any benefit?

(e) It is charged against us, that the Six Companies have
secretly established judicial tribunals, jails, and prisons, and
secretly exercise judicial authority over our people. This
charge has no foundation in fact. These Six Companies were
organized for the purpose of mutual protection and care of
our people coming to and going from this country. The Six
Companies do not claim nor do they exercise any judicial
authority whatever, but are the same as any tradesmen's
or protective and benevolent societies. Neither do these
companies import either men or women into this country.

(f) It is charged, that all Chinese laboring-men are slaves.
This is not true in a *single instance*. Chinamen labor for
food. They pursue all kinds of industries for a livelihood.
Is it so, then, that every man laboring for his livelihood is a
slave? If these men are slaves, then all men laboring for
wages are slaves.

(g) It is charged, that the Chinese commerce brings no
benefit to American bankers and importers. But the fact
is, that an immense trade is carried on between China and
the United States by American merchants, and all the carrying business of both countries, whether by steamer or
sailing vessels, or by railroad, is done by Americans. No
China ships are engaged in the carrying traffic between the
two countries. Is it a sin to be charged against us, that the
Chinese merchants are able to conduct their mercantile
business on their own capital? And is not the exchange of
millions of dollars annually by the Chinese of this city any
benefit to the banks?

(h) We respectfully ask a careful consideration of all the
foregoing statements.

The Chinese are not the only people, nor do they bring
the only evils, that now afflict this country. And since the

Chinese people are now here under the most solemn treaty rights, we hope to be protected according to the terms of this treaty. But if the Chinese are considered detrimental to the best interests of this country, and if our presence here is offensive to the American people, let there be a modification of existing treaty relations between China and the United States, either prohibiting or limiting further Chinese immigration, and, if desirable, requiring also the gradual retirement of the Chinese people now here, from this country. Such an arrangement, though not without embarrassments to both parties, we believe would not be altogether unacceptable to the Chinese Government, and doubtless it would be very acceptable to a certain class of people in this honorable country.

With sentiments of profound respect,

LEE MING HOW,
President Sam Yup Company.
LEE CHEE KWAN,
President Yung Wo Company.
LAW YEE CHUNG,
President Kong Chow Company.
CHAN LEUNG KOK,
President Wing Lung Company.
LEE CHEONG CHIP,
President Hop Wo Company.
CHANG KONG CHEW,
President Yan Wo Company.
LEE TONG HAY,
President Chinese Y. M. C. A.

But alas! these pitiful appeals to the American public and its President, by these "strangers within our gates," were all in vain. Yielding to the demands of this same "balance of power," our Government has grown steadily weaker before it, until now it commands and is obeyed. By its order the most wickedly discriminating laws against the most peaceable, law-abiding immigrants in our country have been passed. I append, in brief, statements of the same. At the demand of this power on the Pacific coast our Government determined in 1880 to send a special embassy to Peking, to secure a modification of the first treaty that existed between the two nations, which secured equal rights for the citizens of either country, in order to enable the United States to abrogate those rights so far as the Chinese were concerned, but holding on to every right of the American in China. Who were the Commissioners sent? John F. Swift, of California, a representative of the element demanding said modifications; William Henry Trescott, a trained diplomatist, who well knew the force of treaty stipulations and the binding obligations of the representations through which they were obtained, and James B. Angell, an accomplished student of public law and a worthy representative of the best element in American politics and society. What did these three distinguished men accomplish? They secured the following.' I quote Articles I. and II. of the treaty. "Article I. Whenever in the opinion of the Government of the United States the coming of Chinese laborers to the United States, or their residence therein, affects or threatens to affect the interests of that country, or to endanger the good order of such country, or of any locality within the territory thereof, the Government of China agrees that the Government of the United States may regulate, limit or suspend such coming or residence, but may not absolutely prohibit it." Article II. stipulates: "Chinese subjects, whether proceeding to the United States as teachers, students, merchants, or from curiosity, together with their body and household servants, and Chinese laborers who are now in the United States, shall be allowed to go and come of their own free will and accord, and shall be accorded all the rights, privileges, immunities and exemptions which are accorded to the citizens and subjects of the most favored nations." The American Commissioners rejoiced over their work, and in reporting it to the Government closed their despatch with the following reference to the action of the Imperial Commissioners: "After a free and able exposition of their views, we are satisfied that in yielding to the request of the United States, they have been actuated by a sincere friendship and *an honorable confidence* that the large powers recognized by them as belonging to the United States and bearing directly upon the interests of their own people, *will be exercised by our Government with a wise discretion, in a spirit of reciprocal and sincere friendship, and with entire justice.*"

These Commissioners, when arraying these *one-sided* conditions, assured the Chinese Government that "so far as those (Chinese) are concerned who, under treaty guaranty, have come to the United States, the Government recognizes *but one duty,* and that is to maintain them in the exercise of their treaty privileges *against any opposition,* whether it takes the shape of popular violence or *legislative enactment.*" How well this confidence in the most sacredly pledged word and assurances of this Government was realized, let the series of legislative acts against this people, and most brutal mob violence, wholly unpunished, testify. In pursuance of these modifications, made under the most solemn pledge of the United States Government that there should be no oppressive legislation against the Chinese. in 1882, May 6, Congress passed an act entitled : "An Act to execute certain treaty stipulations relating to Chinese." The first section of that act was as follows: "That from and after the expiration of ninety days after the passage of this act, the coming of Chinese laborers to the United States, be, and the same is hereby suspended, for ten years; and during such suspension it shall not be lawful for any Chinese laborers to come, or having so come after the expiration of ninety days, to remain within the United States." So that this very first act was not to "limit " or "regulate," but to suspend, and this included "skilled " as well as "unskilled laborers." The Chinese who were in the country at the time this act was passed were excepted from its conditions, and were assured liberty to go from and return to the United States. Still not content with this oppressive act, the enemies of the Chinese in 1884 demanded that certificates should be issued to the Chinese in the country under most solemn treaty conditions, and that these certificates should be the *sole* evidence of their right to be in the country. Again Congress obeyed the demand of these unprincipled rulers, though in direct violation of our honor. Was the hoodlum power content then? Nay! A presidential campaign was ahead, and again they saw their opportunity to still further oppress the Chinese. So the "balance of power " planted itself between the two great political parties, and demanded the most abject and disgraceful act of legislation this Government has ever been guilty of, and be it said to the everlasting shame of both parties that they vied with each other in hastening to obey. In September, 1888, an act was passed by Congress, with a view of executing certain stipulations of a treaty still more unjust against the Chinese, which treaty was signed March, 1888, but afterwards was so offensively amended by our Senate that the Chinese Government did not agree to it. While this treaty was pending between the two Governments, with amendments presented by the Chinese Government not even considered by our Government, the infamous, treaty-violating "Scott Exclusion Act" was passed by Congress in October, 1888. This act provided that no Chinese laborer in this country at the date of its passage, October, 1888, or who at any time prior to that date, had ever been in this country, or who should leave the United States, or had left and not returned, should have the right to return, and moreover it cancelled all the outstanding return certificates which had under previous legislation been issued, entitling those to return who had been here and who had gone away, declaring all such to be "void." A total abrogation and falsification of every sacred pledge this United States Government had given to the Chinese Government of security to and protection of the rights of the Chinese in this country. I here quote again this pledge from "Foreign Relations of the United States," 1881, page 173: "So far as those (Chinese) are concerned who under treaty guaranty have come to the United States, the Government recognizes *but one duty*, and that is to maintain them in the exercise of their treaty privileges, *against any opposition*, whether it takes the shape of popular violence or of *legislative enactment*." Was there any cause on the part of the great Chinese Government for such action? Had it been unreasonable? Had it resented and retaliated because of the insults heaped upon it by our so-called Christian Government? Let Mr. Evarts answer. In reference to this very act he said: "There has not been an approach that this Government has made to China in our domestic interests, in the questions of our polity, the questions of our naturalization, and the questions of immigration, that the great nation confronting us has not met us in the most conciliatory and yielding attitude."

Mr. Sherman said, "the Chinese Government might at once, with great propriety and according to the system of civilized nations, upon our refusing to observe existing treaties, declare that all the treaties are null and void; there is no question about that." Cong. Rec., Vol. 19, p. 8451. The same gentleman said at the same time in his speech in the Senate, "I submit as a national honor whether it be right or proper for us to seek to nullify a treaty that is now being considered by a friendly nation. * * * I frankly say that if our position was reversed, and Great Britain was thus to act toward Americans, I would, without hesitation, vote for a declaration of non-intercourse or war!" Was this "Scott Exclusion Act" legal? I here give my readers the decision of the Supreme Court of the United States concerning it: "The act of 1888, is in contravention of the express stipulations of the treaty of 1868 and of the supplemental treaty of 1880, but as it is in the exercise of a sovereign power vested in Congress, it must be respected and obeyed as the supreme law of the land!"

Mr. Chang Yen-Hoon, the Chinese Minister at Washington, thus most astutely and justly comments on this decision—in an official letter to Mr. Blaine, July 8, 1889. He says "it, the Supreme Court, says that it can not inquire whether the reasons for this action are good or bad, because that court can not be a censor of the morals of other departments of the government, and that the will of Congress must be obeyed, though it is in plain violation of treaties." This able man goes on to say, I should think to the infinite shame of Mr. Blaine, who has sustained all this evil legislation—"you will pardon me, Mr. Secretary, if I express my amazement that such a doctrine should be published to the world by the august tribunal for whose members, by personal acquaintance, I entertain such profound respect. It forces upon me the conviction, that in the three years I have resided in this country, I have not been able fully and correctly to comprehend the principles and systems of your great Government. In my country we have acted upon the conviction that where two nations deliberately and solemnly entered upon treaty stipulations they thereby formed a sacred compact from which they could not be honorably discharged except through friendly negotiations and a new agreement. I was, therefore, not prepared to learn, through the medium of that great tribunal, that there was a way recognized in the law and practice of this country, whereby your Government could release itself from treaty obligations without consultation with, or the consent of, the other party, to what we had been accustomed to regard as a sacred instrument." He then goes on to remind Mr. Blaine that the

United States itself had sought treaty relations with China, and that the Government of the latter had protected and maintained the rights of Americans in China, most sacredly keeping every item of the treaty. The whole correspondence between the Chinese minister and at first Mr. Bayard and later Mr. Blaine, is such as ought to crimson the cheek of every loyal American who has the slightest regard for the honor of his country. Both Mr. Chang Yen-Hoon, and his successor the present minister Mr. Tsui Kwo-Yin, are exceedingly able men. In reading their part of the correspondence, one might well suppose that able, Christian statesmen were trying to induce a dishonorable heathen government to observe the commonest national courtesies—to say nothing of fulfilling its sacred pledges. But all in vain were these expostulations by the representatives of a bitterly outraged people.

Later and very recently, our present Secretary of the Treasury surpasses his predecessor in an oppressive regulation—and that, too, we must suppose from what will appear hereafter—without the knowledge of Mr. Blaine, the Secretary of State, and without notifying the Chinese minister or the Government. I append the correspondence relating to this oppressive order.

Mr. Tsui Kwo-Yin to Mr. Blaine :

"CHINESE LEGATION,
"WASHINGTON, 16th October, 1889.

"SIR :—I have received information, not of an official character, that some new measures of your excellency's Government have been adopted, which it is reported are working hardship to the subjects of China, who seek to exercise the privilege guaranteed to them by treaty stipulations of transit through the territory of the United States." He then asks for information on the subject. Mr. Blaine replies, Oct. 18, 1889, acknowledging the receipt of the above note, and says, "I have the honor to inform you that no new legislation has been adopted on that subject." Mr. Tsui Kwo-Yin replies Nov. 5, 1889, enclosing to Mr. Blaine a *printed* copy of *the new regulation.* He says, "In reply to my inquiries, the Imperial Chinese Consul in New York reports to me that your worthy colleague, the Secretary of the Treasury, has issued a new regulation, requiring every Chinese subject, desiring to pass in transit through the

United States, to cause to be deposited with the Collector
of Customs at place of arrival, a bond of $200, before he
shall be permitted to exercise the privilege *guaranteed* by
treaty of transit through the United States.   *   *   *   I
was much gratified to receive the assurance in your note of
the 18th ultimo, that no legislation had been adopted on the
subject of transit of Chinese subjects through the United
States, and I am at a loss to understand by what authority
the Secretary of the Treasury can adopt a regulation which
has the effect to nullify the treaty. If I have been correctly
informed as to your system of Government, an executive
officer can not enact laws, much less nullify a treaty.''
Quoting our own law against us, he then adds: "It will
be seen that your Congress—which I fear has not always
shown a great regard for treaty stipulations—has passed
no laws which in any degree restrict the treaty privilege
of transit. How then can the Secretary of the Treasury
legally do such a thing?" How, indeed? Yet Mr. Windom
did that thing. Mr. Windom rose to explain. I quote
from his reply, evidently to an enquiry of Mr. Blaine's: "A
question having arisen at one of the ports of the United
States, touching the right of Chinese laborers to enter the
United States in transit from one foreign port to another,
was referred by the Collector of that port to this Department, which by law, regulation and custom, has a general
supervision of such officers and the subjects committed to
their jurisdiction " (he might have added to enforce existing laws but not to enact new ones, "much less to nullify
treaties"). He further says: " Upon consideration of the
question by the Attorney General to whom it was presented, that officer gave his opinion that the right of such
transit was legal and proper." So he was estopped from
forbidding their passage over our sacred soil. But he felt
that he could at least distress them and make their legal
transit as difficult as possible, and so pleading the miserable
excuse—which if true should only have brought punishment to our own officials for neglect of duty, he said "the
Department could not, under the guise of providing for the
transit of Chinese laborers across American territory, have
an open door for the admission, at their will, of such of
them as were disposed to establish themselves as additions
to the population."

But it is evident that he did not feel quite easy under the remonstrances of the able Chinese Minister, for he adds, "Under further consideration *it is proposed to amend* the third paragraph of the regulations of Sept. 28, 1889, by adding thereto an alternative provision, that common carriers, engaged in the business of conveying Chinese in transit, may execute a general bond in lieu of the special bond required in the care of each transit laborer." This interesting information and gracious concession of Mr. Windom was communicated to the Chinese Minister by Mr. Blaine. I quote from Mr. Tsui Kwo-Yin's reply to Mr. Blaine: "You are kind enough to inform me that in consequence of the prohibition of the entrance (immigration) of Chinese laborers into the United States, it became necessary for the Secretary of the Treasury to devise measures to prevent the violation of that prohibition under cover of the privilege of transit. It would seem to be inferred from this declaration that under cover of transit the laws against immigration were being violated. My note which occasioned this correspondence related to the transit between the Eastern ports of the United States and San Francisco. The records of the Imperial-Consulate-General at San Francisco *show that no abuse of the transit privilege has existed since the regulation of Jan. 23, 1883, and it is understood that a report to the same effect was made by the customs officials of San Francisco to the Treasury Department, before the adoption of the regulations of Sept. 28 last,* that is, *that* every *Chinese laborer* exercising the *privilege of transit has passed through* and *out* of the United States *with a single exception,* and *that exception was occasioned by death en-route" ! ! !* Was it in consequence of the one poor man dying en-route and so not going *out* of the country—that Mr. Windom felt the emergency so great as to necessitate such an unheard of order? Did not our *own* customs officials unite with the Chinese-Consul-General in assuring the Treasury Department that all of these terrible people who, in transit, had touched our sacred soil since 1883 had gone out and not added themselves to the population of the country? If Mr. Windom felt that our Republican Institutions were endangered by the presence of this "one exception"—the dead man, he might have issued an order, as legally as his other, to send such terrible exception back to China, and appointed Messrs. Morrow and Mitchell a committee of two to see it done !

The Chinese Minister, strangely enough, did not seem to appreciate the great modification that Mr. Windom had made in his oppressive order, for he writes as follows to Mr. Blaine : " The modification of the third paragraph of the last named regulations, proposed by the Secretary of the Treasury, does not in any manner remove the objection presented in my note of Nov. 5th last. Neither the Chinese Government nor its representatives have any control or influence over the transportation companies in this country, and it is understood that these companies, centering at the port of New York (through which the Chinese residents of Cuba principally pass), are unwilling to give any bond for this traffic. It thus leaves the individual Chinese subject under the necessity of giving the bond of $200. As these subjects are strangers in New York, their only practicable way of complying with the requirement is to make a deposit in that city of the sum named, and as the bond is not released until proof is produced that the subject has actually departed from the port of San Francisco, it is readily seen how great is the inconvenience even in case the subject would be possessed of the ready cash. And in default of this $200 the regulations amount to an absolute prohibition and a plain violation of the treaty. I have no disposition to prolong this discussion by repeating the arguments made in my note of Nov. 5th last, but I respectfully suggest that they remain unanswered by your note of the 6th inst.

" The action of the Congress of the United States in the passage of the Act of Oct. 1, 1888, in the opinion of my Government manifested an open disregard of treaty obligations on the part of the legislative department of the Government of the United States. If anything should occur to make it appear that a *similar spirit* influenced the conduct of any of the *Executive Departments* of that Government, its effect would create upon my Government, I fear, a most unfavorable impression. Knowing the high sense of justice, which marks your excellency's conduct, I had hoped, and still hope, that you might bring about a resolution of this question in accordance with treaty stipulations."

We have now arrived in our discriminating legislation to December, 1889. Was there anything more that the ever alert anti-Chinese party could do to distress the Chinese in this country, as well as in transit? Yes. With a keen eye to their opportunity, and under the direction of that secret power as untiring as death, they saw through the coming census enumeration a chance to drive out, deport or imprison the Chinese who are in this country, under treaty regulation, that as yet with utmost effort they have not been able to utterly violate. Under the disguising title, of " An act to amend an act to provide for taking the eleventh and subsequent censuses," the following act was rushed through the House on the 17th of March last: "Be it enacted by the Senate and House of Representatives of the United States of America in Congress assembled, that the 17th Section of an Act entitled ' to provide for taking the 11th and subsequent censuses,' be so amended as to authorize and require the superintendent of census to enumerate the Chinese population in such a manner and with such particulars as to enable him to make a complete and descriptive list of all Chinese persons of either sex who may be found in the United States at the time of taking the census." The act goes on to order the superintendent of census to provide for the giving of a certificate to each Chinese, *children* not excepted—their parents to receive said certificates, and if *ninety days* after the first day of June, 1890, any Chinese person be found in the United States "without such certificates of identification," he or she "shall be deemed to be unlawfully in the United States and may be arrested upon a warrant issued, upon a verified complaint filed by any party on behalf of the United States, by any justice or judge, or commissioner of any United States Court, returnable before any justice, judge or commissioner of a United States Court, or before any United States Court; and when convicted upon a hearing and found and adjudged to be one not lawfully entitled to be or remain in the United States, such person shall be removed from the United States to the country whence he came, or be *imprisoned* in a penitentiary for a term not exceeding five years." Will the reader please note that these Chinese, thus discriminated against in this infamous act, are in this country by solemn treaty right, and that the proposed certificate was to be the "sole evidence" of their right to be here, their *treaty* rights to the contrary notwithstanding?

This act includes laborers, merchants, travelers, yea, children. A babe born ninety days after the first of June, 1890, would be liable under this beautiful act to "deportation or imprisonment for five years"!!! No one is excepted either that is in the country now or hereafter may enter— for we do not take a census every day; I said no one was excepted—I beg Messrs. Mitchell and Morrow's and their hoodlum constituency's pardon—they did most graciously except the "Chinese Diplomatic and Consular Officers and their attendants;" these gentlemen "shall be admitted under special instructions of the Treasury Department." Mr. Dawes, in the Senate, ventured to ask Mr. Mitchell "what would be the use of Diplomatic and Consular Officers?"— as by this act *all* the Chinese here would soon be deported or in our penitentiaries. Mr. Mitchell shamelessly replied, "I do not know that there is much use for them even as it is now!" The House (Republican) exceeded all its predecessors in passing this wicked act. When Mr. Mitchell was asked by a member whether he was willing for like acts to be applied to Americans in China, he promptly replied in effect, "Yes, there are but a few missionaries and merchants there and they are limited to few places." All of which was contrary to the facts. The churches of this country having large and most important interests in the missionaries, property and many thousands of native Christians in China—all of whom are endangered by these discriminating laws. Moreover, our trade with China is only second to that of Great Britain. But while this act was pending between the two Houses, the Christian people of the country rose in might and protested against any more such disgraceful legislation, warning their representatives in the Senate that if they passed this act they would learn that Christian sentiment could affect elections as well as the hoodlum sentiment of the Pacific Coast. The Chambers of Commerce of New York and Boston sent in their earnest protest against thus endangering our valuable trade with China, which they declared had already been lessened one-third by the discriminating acts already enacted. For once Congress paused in its knee-service to "the balance of power." The Senate proceeded to amend said Act. Their first most destructive amendment was a penalty of $1,000 fine and two years' imprisonment of any census taker who *failed* to give said required certificate. This was maddening enough to the ingenious hoodlum representatives, who, no doubt, had their nice little plan to put in men after their heart who could easily cheat the poor Chinese of their certificates, many of whom could not even know of this act; but when under the pressure of Christian protests, the same honorable body went on its amending way through this last most remarkable act, and actually excepted all children born *after* the taking of the census, and further, all persons other than laborers (why, indeed !) who had met the usual conditions, and finally with one fell swoop of moral victory even over the "political exigencies" of the Pacific Coast vote—no President having to be immediately elected—the honorable Senate actually abolished the "deportation or imprisonment" of men, women, children and babies of ninety days, tourists, preachers and scholars, Messrs. Morrow and Mitchell were in despair, they felt that the very bone, marrow, muscle and blood had been taken out of their protégé; in fact, to them what was left was mere putrid matter, and they hasted to suggest its speedy burial. It was done; but I warn the friends of decency and humanity, to say nothing of national honor and Christianity, that we need to be constantly on the alert, for the enemy is not dead with this infamous Act.

I shall not have completed the record of our disgrace as a nation until I record here a recent Act passed by the municipal authorities of San Francisco which, through local wrongs to many, so utterly violates the Treaty between China and the United States, and withal is so utterly inhuman, that every American should know about it. I quote again from the speech of the Hon. J. W. Foster before the Census Committee of the United States Senate the 27th of last March. He says: "I hold in my hand a copy of an ordinance of the City of San Francisco, which became a law on the 14th of the present month and published in the San Francisco *Examiner* on the 15th, designating a particular quarter in the suburbs of that city as the only permitted residence of the Chinese population, and requiring them, under penalty of *imprisonment*, within sixty days to remove from their present place of residence to the new quarter. Notwithstanding Chinese merchants and other industrious law abiding and peaceable residents have invested

millions of dollars in real estate and established permanent
business in their present locations, they are to be forcibly,
and by the strong arm of the law, driven from their homes.
The attorney, who acted as the city supervisor's counsel and
drafted the ordinance, states, that doubtless the aid of the
Federal Court will be invoked by the Chinese in defense of
their property and business interests; but he says: ' In the
meanwhile there is no reason why the object in view should
not be accomplished if the chief of police and police and state
judges will carry out the law, *without stopping to inquire
what the judiciary* in Washington *may think about it* three
or four years from now.' A bill has been prepared and for-
warded to Congress which, if it passes, will settle for all
time the Chinese question. It provides for the modification
of the treaty so as to confer upon *State* governments the
right to empower municipal authorities to do what the State
constitutions say they can do." That is to say, Congress
is to be asked to pass a bill to allow California to do *what it
pleases* with those who are within her borders, under the
most solemnly pledged *national* protection, and what she
wills to do is finely illustrated in the city ordinance, to force
the Chinese from their hard earned homes.

And now what has been the result of all this wicked work
on the part of our Government? For while we recognize
the power that has demanded it, our Government alone—
whether Democratic or Republican—has been and is responsible for the legislative acts; and they have led to certain
and unavoidable results. Let the parent of children or a
teacher in a school discriminate unjustly against any child,
and how soon persecution from the others follows! The
Chinese have a proverb—" Commit one sin and a hundred
will follow." This has been shockingly illustrated in this
legislative wrong to the Chinese. Robbery, arson and murder, with unlimited persecution, followed swiftly in the
train of these legislative acts. The hoodlum felt the support
of executive authority and has worked his wicked will against
a helpless, inoffensive people. Their helplessness and weakness in our midst ought to have appealed to the commonest
instincts of humanity—but on the contrary, whole volumes
might be written of the most awful brutality, perpetrated
against them, not only on the Pacific Coast but in almost
every Eastern city. A peaceable, quiet, industrious Chinese,

living in a quiet residence street, near us in Boston, had his
windows broken twenty-two times in eighteen months, and
without redress; and the policeman of the street asserted
that he could do nothing.   Three cases of brutality occurred in a single week in the same city.   A Chinese was
working one evening in his own hired house, when a man
threw a stone at him and cut his head in the most shocking
manner.   He was in the hospital for some time in a most
critical condition.   The same night a man's nose was broken
by a cruel blow from an intruder into his house.   In the
third case *six men* went to a laundry where was *one* small
man.   Four went in to do their wicked work, while the other
two remained outside ready to aid, if four cowards were not
able to manage *one* man.   Two held the poor Chinese on
the hot stove, burning his neck most shamefully, while the
other two robbed his drawer of his hard earnings.   Police
were called and refused to do anything.   The same month
a boy stood at the entrance of a laundry where a Chinese
was quietly ironing.   As the man passed by to change his
iron, the boy deliberately aimed a pistol at him, fired, and
just missed him, the bullet entering the counter.   It was
taken out and carried to court, and this time the boy—who
had abused and persecuted the Chinese for a long time—was
arrested and compelled to appear in court.   The act was
not denied, but the judge decided that the boy *was too
young* to *either* be punished or fined !   The boy was in his
teens.   A month later a mob attacked the house of a Chinese
in the same city.   He had a wife and a dear little girl of
three years, who often came to visit my little girl near her
age.   Lillie was as bright, polite and interesting a child as
could be found anywhere.   There was also a baby sister but
a few weeks old in the home.   Imagine the terror of the
poor young mother and her babes, helpless in that great
Christian (?) city.   Chinese friends tried to protect the
home, and one of them was wounded.   When the police
tardily appeared, the only persons they arrested were the
wounded Chinese and one other trying to give aid to his
friends.   Not one of the mob was arrested or ever has been.
The two Chinese who were quiet, peaceable men, and members of one of our Chinese Sunday Schools, were held for
bail over the Sabbath.   My husband was in court when the
case came up, and heard a policeman testify that he found

the wounded Chinese on the ground, and a white man on
him ready to kill him. When asked by the lawyer for the
Chinese why he did not arrest the white man, he replied
"I had to arrest the Chinese to save his life!"   I could
furnish details of outrages against the Chinese in Boston,
New York, Brooklyn, and other places, that would be beyond the belief of most people; and as to San Francisco,
and such places as Tacoma, Denver, Seattle and Rock
Springs, not forgetting San Jose, Sacramento and no end
of places in California, the record of brutality and bitter
wrong in those places is so great, that hardly a lifetime and
many volumes would suffice to tell the tale. The *record is
made* by the great God himself, and the time is surely coming when that same Mighty God, who fears not the "balance of power," has no respect unto the hoodlum's vote,
stoops not to wicked public sentiment as have not a few of
the ministers of God's holy word;—I say the time is coming
when the righteous Judge will *reckon* for all their deeds.
And methinks the time is not far distant when He will reckon
with this Government for its deeds of blood; for every drop
of blood shed in California, Tacoma, Denver, Rock Springs
and elsewhere can be charged back upon the Government,
which not only has not fulfilled its sacred pledge to protect
these helpless strangers in our midst, nor redress their
wrongs, but has on the contrary, by its legislative acts, encouraged and made possible such work. As I recall these
brutalities and the total lack of any protection awarded to
the Chinese by a *Christian people, as a people*, a contrast
great and humiliating, comes before me.

In 1864, on a night that I shall ever remember for its
weary hours of anxious waiting, a Chinese mob went
through the great city of Foochow, of six hundred thousand
inhabitants. Spurred on by evil stories against us, which
had their source in the immoral lives of *foreign* traders,
they had determined to make short work of us. They first
went to our newly dedicated church on East Street, and destroyed it. Then they went to the home of the Rev. C. R.
Martin, of our mission, who lived on one of the highest hills
of the city. Next door to his house, with only the wall between, was a great Tauist temple with its many idols and
priests, poor ignorant heathen who had scarcely heard of
the name of Christ. Mr. Martin had been warned by one

of our native Christians that the mob was coming to his house. Without saying anything to his wife to alarm her, but to be ready for any emergency, early in the evening Mr. Martin went, and, with the consent of the priests, made an opening in the wall between his house and the temple, large enough for them to pass through into the temple. The two little children slept quietly, all unconscious of danger; and not until the mob was almost at their gate did Mr. Martin say, "Now, Mary, we must go." And as they passed into the temple, assisted in this hour of their need by the priests of heathen gods, the mob entered the room we had occupied the previous night, as we had been spending the Sabbath with these friends. All during that anxious night, Mr. Martin, at intervals, as he was able, sent messengers over the wall to us outside the city, with information as to the riot. At last, at four o'clock in the morning, there came to us a scrap of paper torn from an envelope, and on it these words: "The mob is now in our house destroying every thing; but, thank God, we are safe in the temple, and *the priests are very kind to us.*" The morning came, and help was sent our friends; and, ere long, the native authorities arrested offenders. Every cent of loss to natives and foreigners was paid, and our destroyed church rebuilt. Now for the contrast. During the winter of 1881–82, according to the newspaper statements and telegrams, in the City of Denver (a *Christian* city), a mob of evil white men attacked the Chinese of that city. They were as helpless as they had been inoffensive; and, ere any protection was given them, the death-blow had fallen upon one of these strangers in our land.

In September, 1885, a brutal mob ordered the Chinese to leave Rock Springs, Wyoming Territory, within an hour. Defenceless, they prepared to obey; but their tormentors, not waiting for their own limit of time, "growing impatient," attacked them, set fire to their houses, and shot them as they fled,—killing at least fifty, and driving the rest into the mountains to die of starvation and exposure.

Later, came the Washington Territory outrage. And now I ask, in the name of the commonest decency and humanity, where were the Christians, the priests of our God, the temples of Jehovah, in these localities? At this time of the extreme need of these hunted strangers in Denver, in

Rock Springs, in Tacoma, where, oh, where were the Christian homes? Why were not such homes opened to receive these fleeing, wounded, dying, innocent people, with this humane assurance, "You shall be safe as long as we are?" Were the decent American people *afraid* to shelter the wronged? The priests of Tau were *not* in a city of six hundred thousand people.

When the final shots reached their mark, and those pitiful helpless ones fell in the last struggle, at the time of their extreme need, away from their native land, the parents they so much venerate, wife and children, as life went out and the shadows of death settled down upon them, even then did *any* door open to them for a last shelter? Were they welcomed into any temple of our God? Did any priest of the blessed Christ draw near to these dying ones, for whom *he* gave his life, and tell them of the home beyond, of the Saviour our only hope? The record does not read so. In Denver, the "dying man was carried to the *city jail* to die;" his murderers went to no jail, so far as known. In Rock Springs and the neighboring mountains, God's very own lay dead and dying, in the cold and fire, uncared for. In Washington Territory, two who died of exposure that dreadful stormy night, on the prairie, were put upon the cars with the living. And Chinese fathers and mothers, wives and children, are lifting their desolate hearts in an exceeding bitter cry of woe for these loved ones foully murdered in this land; and the great God hears, records, and bides his time. O God, some of us grow impatient, and long for the end!

The San Francisco "Argonaut" sums up the anti-Chinese movement upon the Pacific Coast in these vigorous words :—

"The refuse and sweepings of Europe, the ignorant, brutal, idle offscouring of civilization, meet weekly upon the sand-lots in San Francisco, to determine whether respectable, industrious, foreign-born citizens and native-born Americans shall be permitted to treat Chinese humanely, and employ them in business vocations, or unite with the idle and worthless foreign gang in driving them into the sea."

Deeds of sin, sooner or later bring governments, as well as persons, into most difficult places. This principle has been fully illustrated over and over again by our Government in its wicked attitude toward China. During the latter part of President Cleveland's administration, an honorable Chinese merchant who had lived in San Francisco twenty years, and whose two sons *were born* there and therefore were natives of the United States, was taken very ill in that city, and it was soon evident that he must die. His wife and sons were at his branch store in Victoria, British Columbia. They were telegraphed to come quickly to the dying husband and father. They hastened to do so, but when they arrived at San Francisco were refused permission to land. The Secretary of the Treasury at Washington was communicated with, and a Cabinet meeting, I am told, was actually called, and labored over the solution of this case for some time. Finally they concluded to call it "a case of humanity," and a message was telegraphed to the customs officials in San Francisco to allow the wife and sons to land, and *under official guard* to go to the husband and father, and remain until his death, when the guard should see them back to the steamer!! Under the present Administration and not long since, a steamer on its way from South America, found some ship-wrecked people, among them one Chinese, on a raft at sea. The commander took them aboard and brought them into New York, and all landed promptly save the Chinese, who was refused permission to do so. But what could be done with this human being, whose sole sin was that of being born in China? There was no ship in port to take him to China; he could not remain on the ship; and the law, as interpreted, would not allow him to land. Again resort was had to the Secretary of the Treasury, Mr. Windom, and that gentleman's resources seemed to fail him in this puzzling case. But finally, as there was absolutely no alternative but to allow him to land and remain here until a ship should arrive that could take him away, or to kill him, and as our Government was not yet quite ready to resort to that method of Chinese prohibition—he was allowed, as another "case of humanity," to land, and wait for a ship! Very recently, within a month, two very honorable Chinese merchants of Hong Kong, connected with a great Chinese mercantile house, known in the money centres of the world before we were a nation, came to San Francisco to see their customers. As there is no Chinese Consul at Hong Kong, they could not bring a certificate. They were

promptly refused permission to land in San Francisco, and
although they offered to put themselves under a $20,000 bond
to leave the country within three or four months, they were
not allowed to stay, and had to return to Hong Kong!!
The poor Chinese on Niagara Bridge, last week, without
food or shelter, refused permission either to return to Canada
or to land in the United States, was a spectacle so inhuman
that it did seem as if no lower depth of degradation could
be left to us, and yet—although these wicked laws are thus
strained even to their utmost to distress, torture and drive
out this poor people—Messrs. Morrow, Mitchell and others
annually appear before Congress to urge other laws still more
wicked, ever repeating the old story that the Chinese
are still coming by thousands, more and more, in spite of
law. The Hon. Mr. Foster gave the statistics of arrivals
and departures in his recent speech before the Senate Census
Committee, showing that from Aug. 2, 1882, when the first
act went into effect, up to Oct. 1, 1888, when the Scott Restriction Act was passed, a period of six years, there had
been arrivals 51,261 and 68,974 departures—an excess of departures over arrivals of 17,713. He says: "I have further
an original certificate, signed by the Collector of Customs
at San Francisco, dated the 12th instant (March, 1890),
showing that the number of Chinese laborer certificates,
outstanding on the 1st Oct., 1888, was 20,443. By the terms
of the law passed on that date, these certificates were declared null and void, and the holders thereof were prohibited
from entering the United States. I also have a table giving
a list of all the steamers which arrived and departed from
San Francisco, from and to China, with the dates of arrivals
and departures, and the number of Chinese carried in the
same, from Oct. 1, 1888, when the Scott Exclusion Act was
passed, up to the 14th day of the present month (March,
1890). This table shows that in the year and a half during
which this last restriction measure has been in force, the
excess of departures at the port over the arrivals, has been
9,195."

These facts are well known to the advocates of further
legislation, but they also know that the public generally are
not aware of them. When faced with the fact of this de-
crease at the main port of entrance, San Francisco, they
plead that the Chinese are coming in over the Canadian and

Mexican borders. As there are in all only about five hundred Chinese in Mexico, chiefly merchants, about half of whom went from the United States, and who merely pass through the United States, we are not in imminent peril from them. As to the Canadian border, what between the vigilance of the enemies of the Chinese in the United States and the Canadian authorities, who are profiting by the wicked example of our Government, few, indeed, enter that way. China ceased to make use of her great "Chinese wall" some time ago—having advanced so far as to open her country to foreigners *without discrimination*. I would suggest to our government, in its strait over the three thousand miles of boundary that need to be guarded lest any stray Chinese enter, that a committee be appointed, and again I think Messrs. Morrow and Mitchell (and Dennis Kearney might be added) would be suitable representatives on said committee, to go to China to negotiate for the purchase of said wall to set up along our boundary for our protection against this decreasing Chinese flood !

A dear friend of ours, a Christian Chinese lady of official connections, a lady of great refinement, at whose beautiful English and Chinese house in China I have seen nearly the entire foreign missionary, mercantile and official communities with representatives of our own government entertained in royal manner, is just now visiting with a missionary friend in Ireland, the home of her people's bitterest enemies. She desires to return to China next autumn *via* the United States, to visit her friends here, and to see the people *who sent her the Gospel of Christ*. My husband has found it necessary to write to Secretary Windom to learn how we can possibly secure the entrance of this Christian lady into the country. Is it not time, I ask, for Christian people to move quickly and unflinchingly for the repeal of *all* of these discriminating laws that make such outrages to the Chinese and humiliation to ourselves possible ?

I here quote the words of the Hon. Mr. Foster's able argument before the Senate Committee :

"To-day we can trample upon her [China's] treaties with impunity, and deny her people, within our borders, the rights conceded to the meanest subjects of the most petty monarchy of Europe or republic of America without fear of consequences. But, as I have said, China is beginning to feel the effect of intercourse with Christian nations; she is training her untold millions in warfare and has begun her naval armament. In 1887, our minister at Peking sent to the State Department what he deemed was an important document, an article written by Marquis Tseng, one of the leading statesmen of that country, entitled 'China: the Sleep and the Awakening,' in which he discussed the relations of China to the Christian nations, and pointed out the provisions in the treaties which wounded her susceptibilities, and which she would 'surely and leisurely' proceed to have modified. And the marquis concludes his article with this notable sentence: 'The world is not so near its end, nor the circles of the sun so nearly done, that she will not have time to play the rôle assigned her in the work of nations.'"

It is easy to add that there is absolutely no wise political economy in the anti-Chinese laws. The greatest and most promising future market for American products is in China. The trade of that rich country is yet to be developed. Already American cottons, flour, kerosene - oil, and other products find an open market there; and the future of that market, no one can measure.

The Chinese were partial to Americans, because we did not force the opium curse upon them. We might have had a large share in the development of their mines, railroads, etc., which is sure to come. But as we are now doing, we are not only blocking the way of the missionary in China, but also manufacturing a sentiment against us. In this too shall we reap as we have sown.

The Rev. Louis A. Banks in an able article from Seattle, Washington, hesitated not to declare the truth concerning the horrible outrages there. Writing as he did, from the scene of conflict, his words are weighty. I quote from his article:—

"A few months since, when the news came of the Wyoming massacre of Chinese miners, there had been as yet scarcely a ruffle on the quiet waters of Puget Sound, concerning the now vexed Chinese question. Almost simultaneous with that, perhaps a few days later, there appeared on the scene an *Irish agitator from California,* who proceeded to *harangue the laboring people,* and to organize them into lodges of the 'Knights of Labor.' It has been the old story over again, of the man who was given a small box in which was confined an evil spirit: in answer to its pleadings, he partially opened the box, and out of it sprang a giant which seemed to fill the earth. We had turned loose on us one wild Irishman, and out of his communistic heart has sprung a phantom whose shadow has darkened the whole Northwest coast, and whose tread has made our young city shake with terror. Ere thirty days passed, four Chinese laborers had been cowardly murdered in their beds, and a camp-outfit worth some thousands of dollars burned at midnight, the inmates being driven half-naked into the woods. Within ninety days, these so-called *Knights* arose *en masse* at Tacoma, and drove two hundred Chinese residents from their homes, through the drenching rain, to a railway-station nine miles distant; they herded them on the open prairie, the storm beating all night long on the unprotected crowd, and next morning drove them all into the cars of an outgoing train, except two poor wretches that had to be carried, having died from exposure during that awful night. Seattle only escaped the same or it may be a worse fate by the coming of the United States troops, who arrived in the very nick of time."

(One can't help wondering, where were these troops during the thirty days and ninety days preceding this monstrous work?)

"The mayor of Tacoma, who has brought himself into so notorious disgrace, is a *German liquor-dealer*, who can only make the blindest stagger toward speaking the English language. His family is yet in Germany, and all his money not spent for beer or anti-Chinese demonstrations goes back to the Fatherland. In addition to this, it is an interesting fact, that the seventeen persons, including one woman, indicted at Seattle for conspiracy against the Chinese, are, *without exception*, members of the Liberal League, and enthusiastic followers of Ingersoll.

"There are, of course, some exceptions to this rule, some very sad ones. Notable among these is a Mr. Nixon who was *president* of the Young Men's Christian Association of Tacoma, and a member of the Presbyterian Church. Mr. Nixon's sister and brother-in-law have been for many years missionaries in China, and have just returned to carry on Chinese mission-work on Puget Sound. Imagine their chagrin and deep humiliation upon finding their brother, and

Young Men's Christian Association president, resting under
five well-earned indictments for unlawfully abusing and
driving from their homes the very people to whom they had
come to preach the gospel.

"Now then, let us study a moment the excuses given for
this agitation. . . . We are being overwhelmed by a
great multitude of Chinese laborers, in opposition to and defiance of the restriction law. But the census statistics do not
bear out this statement. *There are only thirty-three
more Chinamen to-day,* when our population is one hundred
and thirty thousand, than there were five years ago, when
we had only seventy thousand people. If *twenty-five* white
people were able to get along peaceably and prosperously in
competition with *one* Chinaman five years ago, there is no
reason to believe *forty-five* white citizens are in danger of
being overwhelmed by the same Celestial at the present
time. . . . The one great bar to the general advance-
ment and prosperity of the Pacific-coast section is that labor
is so high that it practically prohibits home manufacture.
The butter on our table was made in an Iowa creamery.
The lard used to shorten our pie-crust was canned in Chicago. The cheese we eat was pressed in New York. Our
shoes, made from hides which originally grew on Puget
Sound cattle, have twice crossed the continent before they
are ready for our use. The wool sheared from our sheep
this season will be shipped back next year in ready-made
clothing, with two freight rates added. And other things
innumerable might be mentioned. The greatest need we
have is the importation of cheap labor, backed by capital to
sustain manufactories. . . . The Chinaman has one
peculiarity; *he lives according to his income.* If he makes
but fifty cents a day, he lives on vegetable-soup and boiled
rice, and keeps out of debt, and steers clear of the gout. If
he gets a dollar a day, he has beef, pork, potatoes, fish, and
wheat-bread. And if you raise his wages to a dollar and a
half or two dollars, he will eat more chickens, turkeys,
geese, and fruit, out of his wages, than any other class of
foreigners the writer has yet seen in America."

My own personal experience since I returned to this land
has not been of the most enjoyable, up-lifting kind. The
"spirit moves me" to give it to my readers. I have nothing to be thankful for in this experience, save that it is not

worse, as it surely would have been had I lived on the Pacific Coast. For many years we lived in China. At last failing health brought me and mine back to this favored Christian land, the traditional home of the "free and brave." We brought with us a Chinese servant. He was a Christian, gentle, kind, and most courteous to all. On our way home we travelled through many lands, heathen, papal, and Christian. This Chinese servant received not an unkind word or insult in any of those lands. We at last arrived in the United States. We settled for the winter in the parsonage of a church in a city proud of its churches and Christian institutions. Three days after, I sent my Chinaman out with my little boy in his carriage. In an hour they returned with such an unsightly, dirty, hooting rabble after them, that I was shocked, and hastened to bring baby and nurse in. I then kindly told them that I did not want them to follow my baby and his nurse in that style, and requested them to leave.

In return I received only insult and the grossest impertinence. I then told them if it occurred again I would certainly call the police. That ended their coming to our door, for they evidently understood that I would do as I said ; but during our stay of some months in that city, I had no comfort in taking my nurse or baby down town for any purpose, and rarely did I do it save from necessity. On one such occasion I stood in the main street waiting for a car. We were directly opposite an elegant church, with steeple pointing heavenward. The pastor, no doubt, gave his audience sound doctrine as to the brotherhood of man, Christ's love and sacrifice for all, and the duty to love our neighbor as ourselves. Our Chinaman stood admiring the church, now and then making a remark to me. Just then a man passed us. He was dirty and ragged, and puffing a filthy pipe. He evidently had been drinking too much of his native lager or something stronger. As he passed he gave a look of hatred at the quiet, clean, gentlemanly Chinaman standing there holding my baby. The man passed on, crossed the street, then stopped, reconsidered, turned round, and came back to where we stood, and deliberately circled us round and round, with eyes bent full of hate upon the Chinaman, who seemed utterly unconscious of the evil spirit he excited. Over and over again our inspector puffed his vile tobacco in my face.

Of course no police was at hand, and we were only relieved of his presence by the coming of our car.

The last time we went into the street was no better than the first. I went to buy shoes for my baby, and had to take Ka Kü with us. We were again on the main street, and as usual, had a train of ragamuffins at our heels. I took refuge as soon as possible in a large shoe-store, while our escort stationed themselves at the entrance. The proprietor asked me to allow the Chinaman to go into the back part of the store *where he would not be seen,* and then advised one of his clerks to throw water on the rabble at his door. As we emerged from the store, they were ready to receive us. Sick of such company, and with a longing for the *freedom* of China, where I and mine could go abroad unmolested, quite contrary to my intention or wish, I put Ka Kü and baby in a car and sent them home. Such was my *freedom* in that city.

Thence we went to Brooklyn, where we proposed to stay some months if the *lords* of the land would permit. We were in a very respectable, attractive part of the city, near a beautiful park in which I took delight as just the place for my children, since we must be in the city for the summer. What was my experience there? Ditto that in the previous city, only worse. Day after day the rabble followed my Chinaman and little boy. I could not tolerate such associates for them, even if peacefully inclined. But when they followed with vile language, mud and stones, filling our and the neighbors' steps, hanging on the fence and refusing to go, the matter became serious. One Sabbath, Ka Kü and baby came in with hands filled with stones which had been thrown at them, any one of which was large enough to have killed my little boy if it had struck him. For the first time, our patient Chinaman showed signs of annoyance, and then more for the sake of his little charge he so tenderly loved, than for himself; and he asked, "'Teacheress, shall I go after them when they do so?" And I, with an effort, answered, "No, remember the *Christ* doctrine, ' Love your enemies, bless them that curse you;'" to which he assented, and again took up his life of forbearance, and during the four years he remained with us, the patient, loving, Christlike spirit never failed him. My heart has grown hot with indignation many, many times, as I remember these wrongs done, and that these are only *little* things compared with the crimes in the West.

During the stay of our Chinese servant with us, we were accustomed to have our family worship in the Chinese language every other morning, and Ka Kü took his turn in praying. Shall I ever forget his humble, wonderful prayers, his humble confessions of sin, his praise to God for the beauties of his world and the wonders of his grace; touching, beseeching prayers for the gift of the knowledge of Christ to his own people in his native land; and finally and always, his tender, wise, and fitting prayers for me and mine, for the little and older children, and for the teacher and teacheress? I remember one morning he used this expression, wholly his own: "Heavenly Father, help us to hide to-day under thy wings, as the little chickens hide under their mother's wing." And yet the *Hon.* (?) Frank M. Pixley, lawyer of the anti-Chinese party and *their* representative to Congress against the Chinese, says, "They have no souls, or none worth saving." My little boy early learned his part of the hard lesson taught by wrong, and daily said to his faithful attendant in Chinese, "Don't go to the park, don't go to the park! They will throw stones at us." Now, my Christian friends, and especially my *voting* readers, what think you of this experience of mine in this *Christian* land? I purposely emphasize the Christian. I have a perfect right to expect, yea, to demand, at least as much comfort and safety here as in heathen China and India or papal Europe. Yea, I have a right to *more*, just because this *is* a Christian land, the land of the "free and brave," over which the "star-spangled banner" waves; which same banner we shake vigorously in the faces of any Chinese officials who fail *quickly* to redress any wronged American in their country. "To give me to see" (as the Chinese say), I was in a sad plight, compelled by illness to remain in a boarding-house in a big city during the summer, with an energetic, ever-active little boy, to whom our narrow quarters were unendurable for much of the time. All about us were beautiful, shaded streets. Two doors below us was a large, lovely, shaded park, with its extensive pavilion, and great playground for children. It is the site of a battle that was *supposed* to help make us a free people; and yet, so free an American was I, that it was only with much anxiety and care that

I could allow Ka Kü and my little boy to go into those aris-
tocratic streets and shaded park. Is this the freedom and
Christianity for which our forefathers bled? But, answers
one, "It is only rude foreigners that do these things." Hold
on, my friend! My experience is lengthy, but not ended.
If this statement were true, do we propose to allow foreigners to rule and insult the natives of this or any other country while under our national protection? But back of all
these evil deeds is a *sentiment* that makes these deeds possible. I have found it with little American girls six years
old, with boys, with intelligent men. One lady told me that
her son, a lad of twelve, was *indignant* at us for bringing a
Chinaman here, and could not be reconciled to us. This
child-prejudice bodes no good for them nor us.

Finally, I appeal to the press, the Christian people, the
pulpits of this land,—to the press, Christian and secular,
weekly and daily. What are you doing? Where are your
ringing editorials, your fearless denunciations of wrong
and oppression? O ye mighty engines for good or evil, on
which side do ye stand? Few indeed could tell from the
weak, halting, uncertain expressions of many so-called
"best papers;" while many, many, stand openly for con-
tinued wrong, and others keep a *salve-lardum* silence! Oh
for a little moral courage! I appeal to the Christian men
of the country, to the Methodists, Presbyterians, Congrega-
tionists, Baptists, and all the other tribes of Israel. I *know*
that Christianity is not a failure. I draw no conclusions
against Christianity; but I do say, give me an honest
heathenism before a shamming, heartless Christianity.

Christianity is not a failure here; it is not in China. It *can*
make men true, honorable, morally courageous, and just
and kind to all men. Wherever these fruits are wanting,
it is not the fault of Christianity, but the lack of the
true work. No Christian man has a right to plead ignorance, for ignorance that can be enlightened can never excuse a wrong to our fellow-men. Have you, Christian voter,
informed yourself on the Chinese question, or have you ac-
cepted the dictum of your political party? Have you no
responsibility for the hideous wrongs done by men you have
helped put in office? This is "a government for the people, of the people, and by the people." If so, why do not
the *Christian* men hold the "balance of power" between

the two great political parties ?   Why, oh, why ? save that Christian men obey party rather than God.   Oh, the fearful responsibility of the Christian voter !

I appeal to the pulpits.   O ye watchmen on the walls, it is time to cry aloud, and spare not ! This is not the land of our fathers, in some respects other than progress.   I send my son to this country, and do not see him for six years. Annually his photograph is sent me, but when I meet him face to face I would not know him.   And yet those who have been with him these years have hardly noted the changes. Just so is it with our country.   Those living in it, and grow-ing, and, alas ! *changing with it,* are not conscious of the great transformation.   But I am away for years.   The newspapers, like the photograph of my boy, from time to time faintly hint to me of changes ; but I come home each time to find them greater than I could have imagined.   Some of the changes are real advances, genuine progress, bring-ing added strength to us as a nation ; but, alas ! many are the reverse.   I find that less, far less money is expended by all the benevolent institutions in the land, than in the rum-traffic alone.   I find streets once quiet and respectable on Sunday, now the scene of trade and open saloons ; and yet I am assured that this is a violation of our laws.   Where are the officials, then, whose duty it is to enforce said laws, and where the public sentiment to compel these officials to do their duty ?   Ministers, in Monday meetings, are comparing notes as to why the masses do not attend church ; when they have only to look into the empty places in their church pews, and go into the homes of their parishes, and find children, whoso parents as children were regularly taken to God's house, lounging at home, reading doubtful books and papers all the Sabbath day, a Sunday-school service being all they are equal to after a week at school.   Such a gener-ation has come upon the scene, and largely makes up the masses of those who do not attend church.

Numbers are good, and it is said that " figures do not lie."   If, while our church-records are rolling up figures, we are losing in morality, in soberness, in keeping the Sab-bath, in justice and righteousness in our government, in purity and unselfishness in our churches ; if robbery and murder are abroad in the land unrebuked and unpunished, if sin has grown defiant, yea, domineering, and proceeds to rule;—ye watchmen in the pulpits of this land, is it not high time to dispense with polished essays? Let Darwin rest, and even ignore Ingersoll, and call your very own people back to justice and righteousness all through this land!

When members of our churches *talk* temperance, and *vote* rum; when they talk justice, and vote oppression; when they talk for the enforcement of the law, and *silently* see its violation,—it certainly is clearly duty for pastors affectionately but earnestly to find the moral courage to speak out the truth. Such men declaim against *political* sermons; but, if the Christian voters of this land recognized the momentous responsibility of holding the ballot, such sermons would not be needed. But when principle goes down before party even in the church, then it surely becomes duty for the shepherds of the flock to call back the wandering sheep to the fold of safety. Moral courage with the loving spirit of Christ must win all but the *determined* sinner.

For our own safety as a nation, we need to be on the alert, and relax not the strict holding to the principles of justice and righteousness upon which this nation was founded. As things are, *even a woman needs only common-sense* and foresight to dread the future. It may seem a thing so small as to be unworthy the serious consideration of our voters, that Chinamen are insulted in our streets, the laundrymen's windows broken; Yung Ley Teep, on his way to a mission Sabbath school, killed on the street in New York City; years of persecution, oppression, robbery, and murder in California and on the Pacific Coast, and fearful massacres, crime added to crime, and each growing greater, and adding a blacker page to our nation's history. But in the mean while these are *educators* downward, and "strikes" and "dynamite" and communism are of near relation to what we have already had and permitted. The mass of the voters on the Pacific Coast looked serenely on Kearneyism as long as only the stranger from China suffered; but presently it began to be labor against capital, and this looked wonderfully like communism; and then "Committees of Safety" felt it necessary to take a stand for capital if not for men. The same element that persecutes and murders the Chinese is just the very element to make this nation wail in revolution and blood. National crime receives national penalty, and justly. God waited long for us to right the oppressed of this land; but the end of waiting came, and we had our baptism of blood from north to south, from east to west. And can it be possible that the very same generation can forget so soon? The same righteous Judge is on the throne, and again he will reckon with us. May he who cares for the four hundred million souls which he made in China not deal out to our sixty millions all the judgments we deserve for failing so terribly in duty, and in recognition of the exceeding great blessings we have received from his hand, and our corresponding duty toward others less favored!

England has placed an awful obstacle in the way of mission work in China, in forcing the opium-trade on the Chinese Government, and holding it there to the ruin of millions in spite of the wail of agony that goes up from almost every home of that land. France has robbed and wronged China for her own selfish ends. And now our own United States takes her stand with these oppressing nations to block our work for God and humanity in China. We who go to that land, not for dollars, but for souls, stand amazed and heartsick before such obstacles placed in the way of Christianizing the greatest and in many respects the most promising heathen nation in the world. Surely the blotting out three-quarters of the distance separating China and Japan from the United States, by the Pacific Mail steamer line, has a more important significance than simply to expedite the transit of tea and silks to our country, the filling our merchant's pockets, and the increase of our national commerce. The political economist may see nothing more, but the Christian economist must see a far more important result in the placing of the greatest heathen nation of the world beside the greatest Christian nation. Some of us who have gone the old, long, weary way of months on the ocean around the Cape to China, and later over the new way, have appreciated and taken in to some extent the wonderful meaning of the prophet when he uttered these words under inspiration: "And I will make all my mountains a way, and my highways shall be exalted. Behold, these shall come from far, and lo, these from the north, and from the west; and these from the land of Sinim." As if he looked down all the ages into this nineteenth century of light and privileges, and saw that there would indeed be this great highway between the

West and the East, and all nations would traverse it, and only this one nation be oppressed and down-trodden, and the God of the oppressed named *that nation alone by name.* Governments at the bidding of selfishness may make their oppressive and unrighteous laws ; but God still reigns, and his will is sure to be wrought out sooner or later, and his decisions are final. May he not forsake us, but yet save us from the ruin into which wrong and injustice would plunge us ! We have mighty evils to face here, and they are growing. We must conquer them, not by numbers, but by power. And when the Christian sentiment of the nation rises in its strength, and says it shall be done, the God of our fathers will give swift victory.

ESTHER E. BALDWIN.

1218 Pacific Street, Brooklyn, N. Y.

CPSIA information can be obtained
at www.ICGtesting.com
Printed in the USA
FFOW04n1526270217
32908FF

9 781633 912250